THE SOU

FOR GAY AND

LESBIAN PEOPLE

THE SOUL MATE BOOK FOR GAY AND LESBIAN PEOPLE

MICHAEL

SAMUEL WEISER, INC.

York Beach, Maine

First published in 1994 by
Samuel Weiser, Inc.
P. O. Box 612
York Beach, ME 03910-0612

Library of Congress Cataloging-in-Publication Data
Michael
The soulmate book for gay and lesbian people / by Michael.
p. cm.
1. Gay male couples. 2. Lesbian couples. 3. Interpersonal relations. I. Title.
HQ76.25.M52 1994 94-17191
305.9'0664--dc20 CIP

ISBN 0-87728-805-4
MG

Printed in the United States of America

99 98 97 96 95 94
10 9 8 7 6 5 4 3 2 1

Typeset in 11 point Bembo

The paper used in this publication meets the minimum requirements of the American National Standard for Permanence of Paper for Printed Library Materials Z39.48-1984.

Table of Contents

Foreword vii

1. Judgment 1
2. Definition of a Soul Mate 5
3. Are You a Biological Crossover? 11
4. That Special Someone Does Exist 15
5. Your Biological Soul Mate 17
6. I Found My Soul Mate 21
7. Sex Is Good 31
8. Sex without Guilt 35
9. The Nature of Homosexuality 37
10. Nature Holds All the Answers 47
11. Your Ideal Does Exist 51
12. Improving Your Self-Image 55
13. The Power of True Prayer 59
14. The Dynamics of Self-Suggestion 61
15. How Safe Is Your Love? 65
16. The Chromosome #23 Factor 69
17. The Psychology of Homosexuality 71
18. The Nature of Heterosexuality 75
19. Where Can I Find My Soul Mate? 77
20. Attitudes of Church, State and Society 79
21. The Hidden Causes of Human Behavior 81
22. Take Charge of Your Life 83
23. Loving Your Body 87
24. The Magnetism of Joy 91
25. What Is Love? 95
26. The Love and Joy of a Soul Mate Relationship 99
27. What about Bisexuality? 103
28. The Soul Mate Materialization Technique 105
29. The Age of Soul Mate Mergers 113

Suggested Reading and Other Sources 117
About the Author 120

This book is dedicated lovingly to my own beloved *Maria*, and to my most adored son, *John Mathew Michael.*

Foreword

A good third of the letters I have received from the readers of my recently published, updated edition of *Finding Your Soul Mate*, have asked me whether gay and lesbian people also have soul mates. I feel compelled to answer that question as completely and as clearly as possible in light of my own greatly expanded knowledge of this subject.

Hopefully, by the time you finish reading this book you, too, will understand what makes, shapes, or creates a homosexual person, whether he or she resides in a male or a female human body.

Nature will be our wise guideline. Only nature holds all the real and "final" answers to our questions about anything. We may unknowingly trick our minds with false beliefs or with wrong convictions, but nature is never fooled!

Naturally, if you hold on to an "I know it all attitude," then your mind is already closed to learning anything new. A closed mind presents the only "impossible" barrier to penetrate. An open mind, coupled with this new knowledge, can give you many of the answers you need to master your life, to master your thoughts and feelings, and to master your own precious male or female body.

In the spiritual community people are not measured by external socially accepted good behavior. It is only good manners to be open and receptive to new "input" from others. What counts is your internal attitude. If you are closed off to any individual, it is a literal slap in the face spiritually. Being closed to someone is the most rude act any spiritual being can communicate to another.

On the other hand, when you are open to others and to their communication, that is like giving them a big warm hug. That is the greatest compliment you can give another person—your open and receptive posture of being. It tells your spiritual brother or sister that you are a gracious and well-mannered spiritual entity. Your open or closed state of being to another cannot be faked, as in external social interaction when warm appearing handshakes and greetings are masked by hostile and cold indifference internally. You are always known immediately on the inner planes of reality by your open or closed bearing.

My hope is that you will read and think through all of this provocative and controversial material before you make an unwise choice to discard any thought contrary to your present belief system. Take a good look at the whole picture first. Remember, a belief is merely a belief, even though you and many others consider it to be a fact. Your belief might be a fact, as well. However, if not, the truth will set you free from any false beliefs previously held by you.

My own attitudes and beliefs have swung 180 degrees over the past few years, even months. I formerly believed that homosexuality was entirely unnatural! I now know that gay or lesbian behavior is *natural* to the person who is. That will be explained fully in the following pages.

There is not and has not been a human being on earth who has not confused belief with fact. We all have done it. Your own truth is an ongoing sorting-out-process every moment, for you are consistently bombarded and brainwashed with countless ideas and beliefs every day of your worldly existence.

Religion, philosophy, and science err greatly in the haughty and persuasive presentation of "facts" that are eventually found to have really been wrong beliefs.

The only really dependable "mirror, mirror, on the wall" that does not lie is nature. Human mind and human thought can err, and often do, but nature is balanced in the source, and always presents the truth. Hopefully, you will recognize in this presentation that there is a vast difference between genuine objective discernment versus subjective judgment and subsequent condemnation.

Therefore, since this truly is such a controversial social subject, I find it best that we begin our grand journey. We each must be allowed to discern and live our own personal truth. No judgment of others is needed!

I would like to know your candid comments or further questions, so please feel free to write to me in care of the publisher. I extend my warm friendship, my open being, and my genuine love of body, mind, and spirit to all of you!

—Michael

1

Judgment

A judgment always means that the one making the judgment is living the life of the one judged. Essentially, it means that the judge is embarrassed over the way *someone else* is living. It is not possible to judge another unless you are embarrassed about what the other person is saying or doing. This means that instead of living your valuable "life moments" you give them up to live the moments of someone else instead. This is not only a waste of their time, but also a waste of yours. Nothing is more destructive to the growth of your soul than judgment or negative criticism. Judgment removes the sense of individuality.

The progression of life allows each individual to learn discernment. Discernment is not judgment. To observe an act of cruelty and to inform that actor of his or her cruel action is not a judgment, for example. It is rather a valid and objective perception of reality, a true fact. No judgment is involved.

However, if the observer oversteps his or her bounds by telling the cruel actor what he or she has done is wrong, then it would revert back to being a judgment, rather than a discernment. Any accusation or statement of right or wrong automatically assumes judgment. It becomes a subjective, rather than an objective statement. Even the "good old book" of the Christian religion, as well as the "good books" of other religions warn their followers about the danger of making judgments. "Judge and you will be judged!"

When you judge another, it means that you are telling that person that you are a god presiding over him or her. You have chosen to be responsible for this person. A judgment of another implies that you are not responsible for your own life, so you are choosing to be responsible for someone else! It never works. You can try to squeeze yourself into another space and another body, but it just will not fit, for everyone is uniquely different. Thank The Source!

Just think how boring life would be if only one person made all the choices for you and everyone else as well. On the other hand, when you live your own life you will naturally allow others to live their lives according to their choices.

Since each one of us has been literally born into a world of judgment, passed along to us from generation upon generation, almost without end, it will take a very valiant conscious effort to become aware of being in judgment at any given time and choosing to stop it! We were intended to be individual in this reality, not a carbon copy of our loved ones. We did not birth in human form on earth to be judges of one another. We came here to learn discernment, to learn choice and to live truth found in all nature.

Though we have just touched on this subject, enough has been said that any reader would know better than to condemn a person based on his or her sexual choices. The controversial subject of homosexuality has never in my estimation been properly understood and thus addressed truthfully. Let us remedy that, so everyone involved—from church, state, and public—can understand and communicate about the issues clearly. Every human soul on earth is a "fragment" of The Source and deserves respect and honor as such. This journey into understanding gay and lesbian consciousness is best started if you understand that you need to love and honor The Source and your neighbor as yourself.

When anyone is in judgment they are in image. There can be no judgment without an image that is saying the person being judged is not doing something according to the image of the judge. The judge has an image of himself, or herself, of what he or she should be and exactly how to do something that the individual being judged is not doing.

Each judgment you make about another takes you out of yourself and the opportunity to live that moment is thus wasted trying to live life for another being. You are also telling that person they should not be doing something the way it has been done. Every time you use the word "should," you are in judgment. This applies even to telling yourself that you should have done something in another way. You are literally "shoulding" on yourself—or on someone else—and everyone knows that stinks!

When the word "could" is used, it automatically implies the possibility of preference, discernment, or choice. To prefer nonviolence over violence, love rather than hate, allowance rather than rape, life rather than death, shows clear choice and is not a judgment. It is a sign of a matured personality, of taking full responsibility for self-actions.

A victim is always in judgment. When you are not living your own life then someone else is going to live it for you! While in judgment of others, and thus not living your own life, being a victim of all circumstances will seem to be quite real. While when you are living your own life fully, others cannot influence you to play the part of a victim with them. It always takes two, a tyrant and a victim, before that "game" can become your three-dimensional reality. You have moved from a subjective to an objective mode, no longer trying to play god or slave for the whole world.

Judgment remains the largest barrier to being yourself, since you take who and what you are out of the present moment and place you into the life of another, and then condemn them for not being you! When you judge another you do not know who you are. It means you have a weak, or poorly defined personality.

If, on the other hand, you are quite self-assured, but not egotistical, and well-satisfied with self, you will no longer judge others. You will be content to simply be an observer, living your own preferences and allowing all other members of society to live theirs as well. This applies to both heterosexual and homosexual people. We all need to live and let live.

2

Definition of a Soul Mate

Biological soul mates are different than spiritual soul mates, for spiritually a soul mate is the counterpart of any male or female human being. There is only one—and if the original "split half" of yourself was male, your soul mate would be female. If the original split half of yourself was female, your soul mate would be male.

That other half of your whole, holy (or whole-I) being wants to mate with yourself as much as you desire to be mated with him or her. All creations, without exception, are created in a whole or complete form before becoming manifest in the three-dimensional world that we live in. So the true answer to which came first—the chicken or the egg—is the chicken!

Once the creation—no matter what form or species—is created mentally by Creator (or co-creator man), the creative thought is placed into three-dimensional reality and germinates from that seed into full-bloomed physical reality. The blueprint is immersed in *time* and then the "flesh" of atoms, cells, organs, and life systems within that specific idea forms around the blueprint perfectly. Not one atom is out of place or out of balance. This is how every universe, sun, planet, kingdoms of nature and species within them, from mitochondrion and one cell plants to complex insects, fish, birds, mammals to specialized human "containment vehicles" became manifest, or three-dimensional.

The idea is fully within the "nucleus" of the first embryonic atom of any given form. That idea, given "life" or movement through the sustained desire of the given creator, simply builds up the various mediums needed to give the form substance. Perhaps the word "push," rather than "builds" would give clearer insight in this process, since compression is the life-giving force, while expansion is the loss of life—or the death process.

You may note that it takes effort to compress and hold life together—while death is always effortless. It is easy to die. It happens naturally as soon as the desire of the in-dweller of the form, whatever that form, lets go of desire to go onward through space–time.

This is where and why "modern" science errs when it states that an atom draws or attracts matter to it. This same error applies to the view that gravity attracts objects toward the center of the planet. No! It is compression of that mass and everything that falls or is held in its field that creates the illusion and false scientific statements about the source of gravity. A humongous creator is right at this moment in time holding and compressing the whole idea of earth, enriched with the teeming kingdoms of life within and upon it!

All ideas are "whole" when conceived. The One Creator holds the one whole idea of ALL CREATING at the "core" of all existence. We do not use the term creation, for All That Is keeps on creating. It is a dynamic, not a static process. That huge whole idea is divided (and multiplied) into what we presently observe as the entire magnificent "creation" surrounding our sight and senses!

Therefore, the first complete entity-self that is "you" or "me" was first envisaged as a whole human being containing both male and female aspects and attributes. The decision was made by the creating "gods" on Earth (note the small "g"), after creating all of the "preceding" kingdoms of nature as the stage on which we play out our lives. The entity self split into two separate units. One half of the entity would incarnate more as a male and the other half would incarnate more as a female. Meanwhile, the whole entity was always in contact and control of the two halves of self—no matter in what time–space medium of incarnation.

The first "wave" of entities that incarnated came into full formation as a soul mate pair, full-blown males and full-blown females—a perfect match during that first lifetime. However, not all whole entities from the magnetic half of the universe chose to come in on that very first wave. Some decided to wait and see how the experiment worked.

Meanwhile, in the course of time, if one of the original incarnate halves of the entity in female form gives birth to a child, then that child will be one of the halves of one of the second wave of entities who have finally decided to split and incarnate—or that child will be one of the original halves who died and is reincarnating again. As you can understand for yourself, after the first wave of paired soul mates, incarnating side by side, a new factor emerges. As one of the two mates dies as a fully matured adult, and then reincarnates as a child, somewhere else on the planet the original pair of soul mates each go their separate ways on through the hall of time. It is rare that soul mates meet and mate with each other over the course of the many human incarnations. That occurs mainly during the close of the incarnation cycle at individual levels. And it happens for entire civilizations when a closing cycle of the planet occurs—as now in the process here on Earth. This aspect will be pursued and enlarged later. The point to be summarized here is that after the first wave of soul mates paired together, side by side, most other incarnations are void of the physical soul mate interaction.

Note however, at the whole or complete entity level of consciousness, every experience of either split half is recorded as a memory nodule. That is why a bleedthrough might occur from a soul mate who incarnates in another part of the world. You, for example, may feel a great desire to eat a mango or feast on turkey—simply because your soul mate, miles away, is also greatly enjoying a mango or a turkey feast. This applies to moods as well; you may be high in consciousness and feel a sudden down. That low feeling may have passed directly from you to your other half.

Of course, the reverse is likewise true, you may be feeling down and all at once feel greatly uplifted. This does not make you a victim of circumstance—if you think it through—for who is that other half but *yourself*! This split of the entity-self not only allows you to fit into an "animal-form evolution" and breeding pattern, it also allows for a wide range of input over ages of time and evolution of consciousness toward that final incarnation as a "Christed" being, or Ascension into a pure light body.

There is also another soul mate definition which does not concern the split of your one entity into two different halves. That definition is greatly expanded in my best seller, *Finding Your Soul Mate*. In essence, it relates to a substitute soul mate, an interim mate that you will know until consciousness is evolved enough to permit and create engagement with the genuine other half of you.

In order to fully understand the term in that connotation, you will have to know the difference between your soul and your three-dimensional "personality."

Let us first define soul as that inner core of your consciousness. It belongs to the Magnetic Universe and represents the positive nature of your duality. The personality grows out of the Electric Universe, comprised of the trinity of mental thought, emotional feeling, and instinctual action—thus, a mental body, an emotional body, and a physical body. These three-in-one constitute your conscious reality as an individual human being. It is what you call yourself and what you think and feel you are in any given moment.

This personality is the negative half of your expressed duality while in human form—the base of your personal identity—until identity is shifted to the soul within. This is the repulsive aspect of your three-dimensional being. The personality negatively hates, makes judgments, feels guilty and experiences the myriad of other unsavory human attitudes, while a soul-infused human being is attractive and positively allows and senses god within!

When true male/male and female/female mates meet at the soul level, that could also be defined as soul-mating, for their interaction is soul-infused and the love expressed is an unconditional love. These are biological soul mates.

The personality-dominated human being does not know or understand unconditional love, only binding, possessive and conditional relationships. The attitude is, "I will love you only if—you think this way, feel this way, or act this way! That kind of "love" is not love at all. The only love that withstands all time/space interaction between any entities, whether between human with human, nation with nation, or group with group, is unconditional love. Unconditional love can only be expressed when the inner self or the higher spirit or god fragment is present. It comes from perfect balance and security of self within. It is the constant free giving of self, not the unbalanced, taking, taking, taking so characteristic of personality identity.

The homosexual individual can, and often does, find and dwell within that lighted realm of soul, just the same as any heterosexual. Homosexuals can meet, not only at soul levels to form soul mate relationships just as valid as heterosexual soul mate unions, but they also can mate with someone of the same gender at a biological soul mate level. This kind of biological soul mating process will provide gay or lesbian individuals with the same kind of exquisite physical and spiritual joy and sexual fulfillment experienced by heterosexual soul mates. This union—with your own very special biological soul mate—will uplift you and fill your life with the love and passion you long for within your being! It will also reconnect you to a part of you that has been missing.

3

Are You a Biological Crossover?

In some cases a gay or lesbian person may be what is called a biological crossover. In order to understand that mechanism, we simply need to take a look at the creation of existing human forms on Earth.

In the beginning, all God fragments, or entities with human self-awareness, were both male and female within the same "containment vehicle" or spirit form. When the decision was made to incarnate into a gradually prepared human form, the decision was made that these human dense, gross, physical bodies would be divided into both male and female form, like all other "forms" in the three-dimensional electric half of the universe.

Another way of looking at this would be to realize all non-form or non-structural "life"—"spirit"—or "God-fragments" came out of, or issued forth from the magnetic half of the universe. The Magnetic Universe was, is, and ever shall be under the total domain of The Source, while the "passing"—"illusionary"—and "moving" Electric Universe is created as a beautiful garden of diverse life and beauty tended by man and woman.

Man and woman were perfectly designed to be able to take care of the lovely earth garden. Man and woman shared freely in the creative thought and consciousness of The Source. Each "split" half, whether male or female, had equal power, intelligence, and creative talent. Each was free to pursue his or her course in human form.

Despite the apparent "separation" between them, both halves of the whole spiritual entity-self fed in and shared the input of each other into the whole self—during multiple human incarnations into time–space on Earth or on any other inhabitable planet in the universe.

Nevertheless, within the Electrical Universe, positive and negative—or male and female—were different in both psychological and body forms. The sex organs were naturally complementarily different and the purely psychological essences and glandular flows were also dramatically different.

The male portion was modelled to incarnate in a male body, while the female portion was to incarnate in a female form, thus preserving balance in the male/female interactions of bodies, organs, hormone and glandular flows.

However, since both of these "halves" possess free choice, the possibility of a crossover during incarnation is always possible. When a male "half" incarnates at birth into a female body, a great distortion of body chemistry takes place in the unnatural body. The supposedly 100 percent female in consciousness and body has now shockingly (for this is an Electrical Universe) been displaced. The newborn infant grows up with a 100 percent psychological male consciousness in a 100 percent female body. This automatically means that male hormones and glandular flows are dominant in the female form. That person is often a lesbian simply because she is a crossover! Reverse the previous discussion when a female makes a crossover into a male form, and you will understand why a male is "driven" by hormones and glands to play the role of a female, and why a female is driven by hormones and glands to play the role of a male. This is truly a biological crossover in either case.

Let us now assume that you are one of these rare and genuine crossovers, and not one of the psychologically motivated gay or lesbian people. Why in the world would you have deliberately chosen to be a current human crossover?

The answer is clear when you take a true view of history and realize that females have gotten the short end of the stick through most of known civilization. Some have been violated and abused sexually and psychologically beyond human tolerance. In determination to never again go through such inhumane treatment, that female makes the decision to switch over into a male body instead.

On the other hand, the male who has been dehumanized through war after war, pillaging and raping, and always taught to "be a man" even when afraid or needing to cry out—also made the same decision—preferring the female form.

Once incarnated in the physical body, the only recourse is to live out that entire existence, usually torn by "forbidden" urges to mate with the *seemingly* same sex, and being a social outcast if those actions are not approved of by other people in our Western society.

This is especially hard when nothing but ignorance surrounds the "why and wherefore" of the male imprisoned in a female form, or the female imprisoned in the male form. There is a total lack of understanding or any allowance for what a heterosexual thinks is anti-social behavior. So what to do?

Most crossovers realize their predicament very early in life. Most try to ignore or repress their tabooed feelings until finally chemistry overcomes the leash of the mind. Interaction with the same sex is finally covertly or overtly practiced.

Yes, it is true that the male or female homosexuals could eventually gain control over physical lust and transmute it into pure unconditional love for friends, family, and society in general. Many have spent a lifetime trying not to be who they are. That is not what this book is about. As we look into the explanations following, we will know there is nothing wrong with being gay or lesbian. It is natural. A biological crossover does what comes naturally.

If you are one, there is no need for apology to anyone, for you are uniquely *you* and that is all that counts!

4

That Special Someone Does Exist

The universe always maintains perfect balance, so for every star there is a counter-star, for every man there is a woman, and for every woman there is a man. It does not matter whether you are gay or lesbian, nature has already created your male or female counterpart. He or she does exist. He or she wants to be in union with you as much as you want to be connected to him or her! It is natural to love and want to be loved.

That special someone is a grand mirror of your own divine being, perfectly reflecting all your virtues and your faults. He or she loves the things you love and strikes a balanced chord with your consciousness. The two of you are one when united.

Like everything else in life, when you focus in on something it soon becomes your physical reality. When you *know* that you have a unique other someone who is like you, and who is your exact counterpart, you begin to draw him or her to you. This applies to all people.

That special someone does exist for you to love and to receive love given. However, deep within your nature you are either male or female and must have an exact and attractive opposite that balances you. That balance goes far beyond physical expression. It is a sublime fulfillment of your soul.

As we probe deeper into the immense ancestral pool we will understand more fully why everyone can find the man or woman that would be very special in his or her life. Countless of our ancestors have shared incredible love relationships, and in some major civilizations—like the more contemporary Roman era, or the ancient Lemurian era, love affairs between two men or two women were considered normal and no adverse social stigma was attached.

Our DNA and genes have far more impact and control over our lifestyle than we would imagine. All the great love matches recorded and living in your genes will allow you to re-create any one of them at your desire—and when you have the knowledge of how to do it. By the time you have completed reading this book, you will be well equipped to attract the most desired "dream lover" into your own physical life. Your very own special someone does exist. He or she is known fully by you in your DNA or genes. He or she is someone that has loved and been loved by someone like you in the past—the perfect match. Your body chemistry holds the hidden key here.

The generally believed false belief that you are alone without anyone to love, or without someone loving you fully, stems from guilt and deep feelings of unworthiness. These negative feelings form layers of webbing that hold you a lonely prisoner within them. These false beliefs need to be seen as the erroneous convictions they are and peeled away, one by one, until self-worth and self-love return to you.

That special someone, your spiritual or biological soul mate cannot break through into your specific time-space field when self-doubt and self-depreciation stand like thick stone walls between you. Tear them down!

Hopefully, if you do not already possess self-worth and a genuine love for who and what you are, that will come back to you, along with a special someone, after reading and applying the "how-to-do-it" techniques in oncoming chapters.

I know and love who and what you really are. You alone create your joyful or sorrowful destiny. Go joyously into your future knowing confidently that your own special someone is waiting patiently for you to appear in his or her life, as well!

5

Your Biological Soul Mate

Your body chemistry is the basis and key to all of your physical movement. Control the chemistry and you control your movement. This again, is easier said than done. There are well over 20 billion of your ancestors literally still living in your DNA and genes. Your seemingly unique thought and feeling generated from everyone you encounter everyday arises, as a rule, from your body chemistry. You act and react to every single person or group in every life situation according to the living attitudes, and therefore, the living "messages" of your countless predecessors, just as each one of them likewise responded to their dominant genetic codes during their "day in the sun."

Like it or not, your body chemistry tells you exactly how to think and feel about everything. This means that "freethinkers" are not as free as they think!

We are ONE because each one of us holds the genes and DNA of everyone who has ever lived on Earth. All of them are faithfully recorded in every single cell of our bodies. This explains why our bodies are so much more wise than we are. They hold all of the wisdom of the ages.

Naturally, our present parents and grandparents pass along to us the most dominant "programs," signals, or commands of response. In fact, our last seven generations, and more prominently yet, the last three generations, affect our thoughts, feelings, and actions the strongest. We may think and feel all we want that we are making the final decisive choice to act or react through "our" mind, when in reality, our ancestors are doing almost all of our thinking and our feeling for us. This is a truth that is very hard to accept by most of us. Our egos like to think they are the big boss! We all like to think we are the captain of our own ship!

Where, then, are "you" in this past and vast sea of squabbling voices within your being? Paradoxically, the only time that all of these teeming voices within you can speak in unity, with *you* as sole director of thought, feeling and action, is when your ego is calmed and set aside. *You* then are the unity and automatically respond as a whole person. This may be the real meaning to (whole-I) holy being! As a whole self, you are safe and secure in all your worldly interactions. Meanwhile, each ancestor living in your being tries to be the number one, the strongest entity, and tries to be in charge of your body's actions and reactions.

Since most of us have a long way to go before we truly know the intimacy of self, or can find safety in all our worldly interactions, we must remain under the dominance of our more powerful DNA and chemistry of our genes until then. We are still countless divided selves!

How does all of this concern your biological soul mate? Simply by the fact if your dominant resonances or reactions to any individual you encounter match the deeply loving relationship of one or more of your more dominant ancestors, and his or her idyllic marriage or love affair, that newly encountered individual can and would support a similar loving soul mate kind of relationship with you today! That person could join with you as a biological soul mate. He or she fits the characteristics and aspects of that great love match known and savored by your current foreparents, or within your seven last generations—or possibly even by one or several more distant but more dominant ancestors. The main point is that the new person in your life has vibratory frequencies and patterns identical to a past loved one by a past ancestor.

Once such a great love affair is deeply imbedded in the DNA and genes of any one link in your ancestral chain, it will automatically draw you to that same joyous blissful vibration today. When that special someone enters your conscious sphere you will know it! You will think it, feel it, and react to him or her with that same kind of feeling of love and affection. At the same time, during the duration of that soul mate love affair, you will add your own distinct and unique tone, note, or frequency vibration to that relationship.

When biological soul mates unite, they are tremendously supported in their love by their bodies. Both of their DNA and gene pools are deeply impacted with grand feelings of love, respect, and caring so blissfully known by their blessed ancestors, and now resounding within them. Love is the greatest gift anyone can give another.

Your own life unfolds or manifests according to the following perpetual and universal formula: whatever is focused upon by your mind is recorded AND REPEATED. Therefore, your love breeds love. Your hate breeds hate. Your abundance breeds abundance. Your poverty breeds poverty. What you live is relived in your being, forever and ever and ever. When you curse, curses fall upon you. When you give thanks and feel appreciation, thankful and appreciative events follow you.

When you realize and utilize this great Law of Being by consciously choosing to dwell upon abundance, love, pleasure and safeness, then false insecurity, lack, pain, and hate will disappear from your daily life. It is universal law!

You may realize now that your instant feelings of like or dislike for someone new that you meet stems directly from your body, not from your mind! Your genes are telling you to greet someone warmly or coldly within you—even though you may greet them warmly socially. After truly getting to know this person, you may realize that your first chemical impression was prejudiced and totally unjustified. This also applies equally in reverse. Someone you first meet may arouse warm feelings that may prove to be quite undeserving in the course of due time.

A biological soul mate encounter would be a rewarding experience, not only for you, but for posterity. If you are eager for that kind of love and romance, you are on the verge of knowing and utilizing a proven formula for success. Use it!

Somewhere, sometime, perhaps many places and many times, one or several of your ancestors personally knew a grand and fulfilling love affair. Your focus on that thought, with intense desire, can literally unearth that same vibration within you. Once your own unique consciousness is vibrating at that frequency you will begin to draw that special someone to you. Energy follows thought! What you put your focus upon mentally with strong feeling must eventually "re-live" itself within your own individual being. Bless you, and your someone special.

6

I Found My Soul Mate

To read about it is one thing and to do it is really quite another! I found my soul mate. The pursuit began in dreams and ended in a dream—or with a dream, quite literally.

At that time in my life I was living in Virginia Beach, Virginia, drawn there by a deep interest in the amazing works of the great clairvoyant, Edgar Cayce. Though Edgar had made his exit from the living zone, the Association for Research and Enlightenment, or the A.R.E. library, located in Virginia Beach, contained many thousands of pages of his illuminated insights and I studied these records for a period of several years.

During my first few months in Virginia Beach, I met a truly amazing psychic named Mikey. During a social visit with Mikey I confided in her that I had been meeting my soul mate in my dreams. Mikey asked me to tell her about it, so I explained that for almost two years I had been meeting, talking to, and holding my soul mate in my arms in my dreams.

When the first dream encounter occurred with her, I thought she was Bonnie, a greatly loved "special someone" I had loved and lost years before. However, I soon realized the energy was different, it was not Bonnie, but someone I did not know yet.

Having learned the immense power of self-suggestion, I decided that rather than dreaming randomly about this lovely female, I would simply give myself a very strong suggestion, just before falling asleep, that I would meet her in my dreams that particular night. Sure enough, it worked perfectly. That night I had a most wonderful encounter with my dream girl. I awoke quite thrilled with the vivid memory of our amorous meeting in dreamland. The feeling of joy over that sweet encounter would permeate and last through my entire day. Therefore, my nights were filled with romantic adventure and my days with loving memories. However, I was beginning to wish that my dreamgirl would become a physical reality in my life. I asked Mikey if she had any psychic impression of when my soul mate would appear physically in my life.

Without hesitation, Mikey said that she knew my soul mate would materialize physically in my life within six months. A thrill of joy shot through my being and I gave Mikey a big hug and thanked her for that welcome message.

Six months later, while working at the *Virginia Free Press*, a small newspaper I had founded, the phone rang and I picked it up to answer.

"Hello," a lovely female voice sounded. "Can I put an ad in your paper over the phone?"

"You sure can," I responded, always happy to get any additional income for my fledgling newspaper. "What is it," I said, grabbing a ballpoint pen to take down the ad.

"A thirty inch painting of your dream for fifteen dollars," she said.

"What?" I said, not believing my ears. "Are you telling me that you actually paint someone's dream?" What kind of a girl is this, I mused.

"Yes," was the instant reply. "And I dance, act, sing, and do many other things," she added.

A "button" deep inside of me seemed to have gotten pressed. Why did this voice seem so familiar? I felt a very strong urge to meet her in person.

"Can you bring the ad to me in person?" I asked. "It will be three dollars."

"Of course, how do I get there? I am at the A.R.E. headquarters on the beach."

I gave her clear directions on how to get to my office—in my home, and told her I would be waiting since I had to get the paper ready for printing. Less than an hour later I looked up from my desk to see the girl of my dreams walking up to me with a big smile.

I smiled back and looked long into her eyes and then finally blurted out that I already knew her—that she was the soul mate I knew would come into my life.

Pam looked startled. She shook her head negatively.

"No, I have already met my soul mate. His name is Karl. We just met at the A.R.E. this afternoon."

It was my turn to be startled. However, I kept myself amazingly poised and at ease, despite her astounding and greatly disturbing announcement. I refuted it immediately.

"No. I know for sure you are my soul mate. I met you in my dreams. It's you, I know!"

I continued as she stared back at me, "You are just fooling yourself. I know a whole lot of people who have tried to make soul mates out of someone they were attracted to. It just doesn't work."

Pam continued her strong denial. Then she suddenly changed the subject.

"Here is my ad," she said, "and here is the three dollars. When will the paper be out?"

I smiled at her wise and sudden shift of focus. I told her the paper would be out on the coming Wednesday afternoon.

Now the subjects changed rapidly as I quizzed her, question upon question about where she was from, when had she arrived in Virginia Beach, and what had prompted her long trip to this part of the country.

Pam explained she had driven practically straight on through from her home state to Virginia Beach. Her trip took her three days. The major reason she had left her state was because she knew positively that her soul mate would be here in Virginia Beach, near the Edgar Cayce Foundation, the A.R.E. She had just arrived early that day.

I smiled another huge smile again when she admitted that she had driven all the way from her home state for three days just because she knew for certain that her soul mate was here in Virginia Beach. I gave unseen and silent thanks that she had heard my "broadcast" telling her where I was at!

Somehow, I was wise enough to back off from pushing the fact that I was her soul mate, and that she had just verified it. Instead, I kept on with the small talk for about an hour when Pam suddenly realized that she had to keep an appointment to look at an apartment for rent, just a few blocks down the street.

I was strongly tempted to tell her again that she was my soul mate and could move in with me. My home was huge and I was alone except for one bedroom that I had rented to a male friend, but I held my tongue.

Before leaving, Pam smiled brightly and told me she had really enjoyed visiting with me, and that I "had an interesting face," and that she would love to come back for a further visit with me on the afternoon of the next day.

My heart jumped! I knew that a small fragment of her unconscious being must have recognized me. I assured her that I would be very pleased to have her stop back for a visit anytime!

When Pam left, I sat back down and replayed our conversation together for a long time. I wondered who Karl might be and I felt a little trepidation, but I swept it quickly away with the sure knowingness that my soul mate had finally arrived. It was indeed, Pam, even if she had not yet fully recognized me as her dream lover who had summoned her to Virginia Beach.

Sure enough, the next day Pam stopped by again for a long chat. She announced with a smile that she had rented a small, but cozy and fairly inexpensive apartment and was very pleased with it.

We talked for well over an hour. When Pam stood to leave, I arose and reached out for her hand, but she quickly stepped back out of my reach and told me she did not want to "rush things."

I quickly apologized for being so forward—but told her it was just my nature to be warm and friendly. However, I would respect her wishes and would not press my "attentions" on her!

Pam suddenly mellowed. She took my hand and told me she had again enjoyed talking with me and would stop by again the next day if that was all right with me. I told her I had enjoyed visiting with her, too, and would be happy to see her on the following day.

Holding on to the good mood, I walked slowly with Pam to her car and opened the door for her to get in. Pam thanked me and slipped behind the wheel. She looked so beautiful and I stared wordlessly at her for a moment.

Pam started the car engine. She looked up at me and seemed suddenly startled. Her face paled and she let out a loud scream. I stood looking on, wondering what in the world was going on with her.

"How did you do that?"

"Do what?" I said, puzzled by such an odd question and her sudden hysteria.

"Change your face—change your face like that!" she screamed.

"What do you mean—change my face?" I asked in pure wonder.

"*Your face changed*! You were somebody else, somebody I seem to remember." She answered, still very uptight and talking louder than normal.

I suddenly realized that Pam must have seen me when we were together in another lifetime and I felt relieved that the problem was solved.

"Pam," I said gently, "you must have seen me when we were together in another lifetime. I didn't do anything but look at you. Soul mates often share lifetimes together."

My calmness carried over to Pam. She relaxed a little, though she was visibly shaking and still appeared to be in a state of shock. She struggled to speak. I squeezed her hand and told her all was well—and that I would see her tomorrow.

Pam nodded slowly and managed a weak smile. She backed up her car and waved a fleeting goodbye, but I could sense that her mind was not on her driving.

I now know in retrospect that all reincarnational "recalls" spring up from an opening in our second brain—the "light brain." All of our lifetimes are lived simultaneously in the ETERNAL NOW. However, our light brain keeps perfect track, or an exact record of all of our special light "fragments," or our lifetimes—and our many faces and individual experiences of you or me as the whole entity light-self!

The next day when Pam arrived for her now usual visit she seemed to have dropped a lot of her walls. When I asked her if she would like to go out to dinner with me that evening, she accepted my offer right away.

I arrived early at Pam's little apartment. We went to a fine restaurant on the beach and enjoyed a great meal together. After dinner, Pam suggested that we take a leisurely stroll along the boardwalk beside the golden beach. It was a full moon evening and magic seemed to be in the air. The temperature was perfect and we were both in a light and airy mood. As we strolled along, we both noted and remarked how harmonious our stride was together. I had the distinct feeling that we had walked together on many paths before.

The bright golden moon enhanced the golden sands of the beach and the ocean was unusually calm and deep blue. My whole being and spirit was caught up in the romantic spell of the night. Suddenly, I felt a strong urge to share my most significant soul mate dream with Pam. That particular dream evolved around my deceased brother Richard. I told Pam that I wanted to share an important soul mate dream that I had about three months before I met her. Pam encouraged me to go right ahead, so I began to tell her my amazing story.

First of all, I gave Pam an insight into the background for the dream.

My brother Richard, a young, middleaged and seemingly healthy person, suddenly died of a heart attack only a few days before the dream. I already knew through my own very real and personal "death experience" at age 18 that there is no death! There is simply a transfer of conscious awareness out of physical body mass into spirit body. I knew Richard had just "stepped out of sight" so to speak, but was alive and well in the less dense spiritual world of existence. Nevertheless, I was greatly surprised and tremendously disappointed. I had never really taken the time to sit down and tell Richard what an incredible and ideal role model he had been for me—what honorable and high ideals he had set for me through his joyous and winning ways. It seemed too late to deliver that message now!

However, through a great thirst for knowledge and strong self-discipline, I had learned the technique of self-suggestion to the point I could suggest and dream at will, not only about my dream-girl, but about almost anything or anyone I wanted to dream abut strongly enough.

The technique was simple. I quieted my physical and mental being for a few minutes, and rested emotionally in a calm, gentle space. Then while in that semi-awake, semi-asleep focus, I would mentally and emotionally project a highly charged self-suggestion that I would dream about that thing, or that person.

This time, though, I was about to give a new twist to that process, I would use the dream state to bridge over into the spiritual reality where my brother Richard resided. I knew that my brother, who was now in his spirit form, was still probably close to our earth plane. Therefore if my desire was strong enough—and it was—through self-suggestion I could go through the "back door" and meet with him and communicate my love.

I charged myself with intense desire, and after several poignant and power-charged suggestions to meet my brother Richard in a dream sometime during the night, I fell into a restful sleep.

Suddenly, I was fully awake in a very vivid dream reality! My soul mate and I were sitting side-by-side in a sleek, long, black hearse. A man and a woman sat in the front seat. We could only see the back of their heads as both of them were facing forward. The man was the chauffeur. He drove our car right up to a high gate which slid silently open before us. He stopped the hearse, turned it completely around, and backed it into the opening. I noticed that he parked the vehicle exactly halfway in the gate and halfway out. The back of the car was now on the *inside* of the gate, while the front half of the vehicle remained on the outside.

My soul mate and I both jumped quickly out of the car and stood hand-in-hand, waiting. We did not wait long. A bright light appeared in the distance and moved rapidly toward us. I knew it was my brother Richard. I let go of my soul mate's hand and ran excitedly toward my brother.

As the light sped closer, it transformed shape into the familiar physical human form and broad smiling countenance of my beloved brother Richard.

We shouted loud salutations to each other and embraced warmly with strong hugs—while clapping each other on the back enthusiastically! It seemed like we talked for hours. I was able to tell my wonderful brother how much I had loved and admired him—and how he had been the best ideal person that any brother would want to emulate. Richard accepted my praises humbly, true to his grand character.

All at once we both knew that "time was up!" We exchanged final goodbye hugs.

Suddenly, Richard materialized a large basket of assorted fruits and handed them to me. He told me that my body lacked vitamin K—and that if I would soak dried applies in a cup of water every night and drink it on the next morning, I could soon balance and restore my health.

I knew I had to go back to the gate where my soul mate waited immediately, so I gave Richard a final hug and expressed my thanks for the fruits and advice and raced back toward the car.

My soul mate grabbed my hand and we both jumped very quickly through the door into the back seat. The driver instantly started the car and pulled forward out of the gate.

At that exact instant the car vanished! My soul mate and I were now flying swiftly through the air on what appeared to be a long flat surfboard. The starlit night sky was beautiful and a full moon shone overhead. A warm tropical breeze rushed over and through our beings. We were sailing thousands of feet above a gorgeous golden beach framed by a deep blue ocean. There was magic in the air!

My soul mate seemed to be piloting the "ship." I decided I wanted to snuggle closer to her, and as I did, the feeling of love and ecstasy now surging between us was blissful beyond description.

At that point I snapped awake. That incredible dream excursion was fresh and clear, and I recalled and relived the dream again and again until it was indelibly imprinted into the atoms of my being!

I paused from my long dialogue to look down at the rapt face of Pam. We both stopped walking. Pam spoke in a low and soft voice, asking me to tell her again how long ago that I had dreamed that dream. I repeated that it had been approximately three months before she had arrived in Virginia Beach.

Pam nodded silently and then began to walk with me, hand-in-hand, toward the city again. Neither one of us spoke. A warm soft breeze and a moonlit night of great splendor surrounded us. There were other lovers strolling along the boardwalk, too, but I hardly noticed, for my heart and soul was filled with love for Pam.

When I dropped Pam off at her apartment, she looked openly and warmly into my eyes and asked me if I would like to come over to her apartment for dinner on Friday evening. I squeezed her hand, still keeping my distance, and told her I would love having dinner with her every night—but that if I had to wait two days until Friday I could manage it.

Pam chuckled and slipped through her door and waved me a warm goodbye. I waved back with another wide smile on my face. I drove home that evening feeling like something tremendously wonderful and dramatic had happened—but I just could not quite put my finger on it!

The following day passed without a visit from Pam. I knew that I would be seeing her at dinner the following night, but I yearned for and missed her greatly. At the same time, the intellectual part of me wanted to play "hard to get." I was torn deeply by the desire to go to Pam's apartment immediately upon finishing my work on the paper—and the desire to play hard to get—to keep my distance.

However, emotion always wins over mind when body chemistry rules. I finished work and soon found myself starting up the car and driving elatedly toward Pam's apartment.

When I arrived at her door, Pam was surprised but obviously pleased to see me. I was not aware of the very astounding surprise that awaited me.

I sat down beside her on the couch and after a few minutes of catching up with each other, Pam suddenly dropped what was tantamount to a nuclear bomb. She took my hand tenderly and looked deep into my eyes and announced that she knew she was my soul mate.

My heart pounded as she explained that she had dreamed the same dream of me and my brother Richard. She said she had felt very worried about me while she waited at the gate for me to return. She added that she thought I might not return in time for us to go back to our physical bodies. She explained that when I began telling her about my dream she had decided to hold the knowledge and experience until she had taken the time to adjust to it—and that she had been thinking about me all of the time and was wishing I would come to her.

At that moment I could not withstand my overwhelming urge another moment. Pam felt the same—we merged into each other's arms with a passionate embrace. The feeling of ecstasy racing through every cell of my body was ecstatic beyond belief. The great dream love we had both manifested on the inner planes became a physical reality that night—and days to follow.

I desired my soul mate, and I found my soul mate, and so can you! The seemingly long wait was well worth it!

However, there are many kinds of and more than one soul mate for everyone. Over a period of time, after the courtship period while we were both putting our best foot forward it became very apparent that we were heading in two different life directions. We had both found a needed fulfillment—yet we knew there was more beyond what we could share together. We gradually released our "hold" on each and parted our individual ways again.

Over the years that great unfulfillment within me has been fulfilled greatly! I am once again enjoying with all my heart and soul an ecstasy-filled soul mate union—with my lovely soul mate who came from a far away country to find her equal in America. We are perfect mirrors for each other and the daily job and spiritual growth we share together is beyond words.

If we can do it—and others are doing it—so can you! *You can find your soul mate, too*!

7

Sex Is Good

Sex is good. Sex is great! Sex is fun! Sex brings back the lost magic in our lives. Sex is tremendously good for the physical body. There are three things that help to develop the size of the neurons in our bodies, kundalini rising, tactile sensory perception, and sex. Joy is also extremely healthy for every nerve and cell of the body, but joy goes deeper than chemical neurons and cellular structures; it imbeds or imprints the very atomic levels of our physical being.

Pure rage also overwhelms the nervous system and develops the length of the neurons. However, most people dilute rage down into anger—which is comparable to the feeling of guilt. Both anger and guilt take away from rather than add to good body health.

Meanwhile, we are constantly barraged by a bewildering barrage of "thou shall or thou shall nots" with the "thou shalt not" leading by ninety-five to one.

From stern religious perspectives sex is only meant to be used for reproduction. However, orthodox Western religion errs more often than not. Sex is something infinitely spiritual and healthfully balancing to both body and psyche.

All particles and forms of nature contain both male and female sexual polarities within them. Sex is the most natural and body pleasing act in nature. It is not sinful! Sex is exciting and stimulating. Sex lifts the body, the mind, and the spirit. Sex can make your neurons grow and keep you young, vital and healthy!

Sex is not bad, it is always alive and responsive within every one of us. If you quiet your being, and feel your sexuality, you can feel the deep undercurrent of electric pulsation in your sexual center. The rate of pulsation will vary in speed and intensity from day to day or moment to moment. However, it is always there as long as you are alive in your physical body.

With practice you can tune in to your sexual energy and turn that exquisite vibration into making love to your own cells of your body. That is the very highest use of your sexual vitality.

Meanwhile, you can give your body a great lift every time you "make love" whether to yourself or to your sexual partner. Sex is good and do not let anyone tell you otherwise.

In terms of nature, in many countries and cultures people practice sex with a whole harem of others of the opposite sex, a man with many "wives" and a woman with many "husbands." Sex was also practiced between partners of the same sex way back in ancient Lemuria during the great Atlantean civilization that followed, and in more recent history, during the Roman empire. Sex between members of the same sex was common in Rome and not considered unusual or wrong.

Though the original design after Chromosome #23 was for male to be with female and female to be with male, there was never any intent that monogamy would be the rule (or the law, as it now is in most countries of our "modern" world). Nature requires that all things must change or die. Sexual partners will have a long and enduring relationship as long as both partners are changing in the same direction together and growth between them is constant. Otherwise, they will reach the end of the relationship and move on to new paths and other relationships.

Nature is the final judge in all relationships, not man or woman. Nature blesses (unites) the good relationship and curses (separates) the bad ones. Our contemporary Western social structure essentially favors one-to-one heterosexual relationships, but we all know that this is an "ideal" and not what really happens. A gay or lesbian person is often considered out of step with society. However, the good relationship is one where two people give each other joy and happiness and the unhappy relationship, whether heterosexual or homosexual, is the "unholy" one.

Sex is good. Only a dirty mind finds sex dirty! Sex is yours to enjoy for the rest of your natural and wonderful days in this blessed human body. Enjoy it!

8

Sex without Guilt

Guilt has more control over our lives than we might ever realize. Guilt literally permeates the atmosphere of every walk of life on earth. Guilt is heaped upon us, both intentionally and unintentionally. We rarely encounter a free-wheeling, guilt-free individual in our "civilized" culture.

Sex without guilt is even more rare. From an early age we are consciously or unconsciously taught to view our natural excretion functions as dirty. We are covered up hurriedly and told that we must not show breasts or sexual organs publicly. If we do, guilt is heaped upon us. We grow up feeling guilty about our sexuality and our sexual needs. By the time we reach physical maturity, our manhood or womanhood is scarred with guilt.

Sex is not only good, but it must be guilt-free if it is to bring health and balance into our precious human bodies. Guilt-free sex means that you honor and respect your own divine physicality and sexuality, as well as the divine physicality and sexuality of your sexual partner. When your sexual interaction shows honor and respect for the divinity in your partner you will be enjoying sex without guilt.

Sex without guilt exalts you and your sexual partner. Sex without guilt means that you value your own self-worth and the self-worth of your mate. Sex without guilt is the natural order of life. Sex is to be enjoyed, not avoided. Sex without guilt will make you an outstanding and desirable sex partner. When you are light and filled with the fun and easy flow of life you are guilt-free. You stand out like a bright light in a dark guilt-laden society because you are a bright space in the lives of those you touch!

Guilt weighs you down, while a light and carefree spirit exalts and lifts you up. Sex without guilt means you are awake and know who and what you truly are. It means that you have finally learned to live your own life—not for the life or values of some well-intentioned but often ignorant friends, loved ones, or advisors.

Let the spark of light and joy fly when you are sexually aroused or engaged. Sex was never ever made to create or harbor guilt with it. Sex was good from the start and is good now and will always be good—and sex without guilt is even better!

Take or make the time to sit down or lay down with yourself and examine your sexual attitudes. If you feel the slightest guilt about your sexuality find out why. Trace your thoughts and feelings as far back as possible through your childhood to see how and why you accepted or determined sex was not innocent. Your ancestors may be expressing loads of guilt through your DNA and genes, but that guilt feeling is only yours if you accept or agree with it. If you agree that you must feel guilty about any sexual interaction, then trace back to where that faulty belief began. You need to break loose from unnatural feelings of guilt, and knowledge will do that for you. Knowledge gives you back the freedom of choice, the freedom to change your mind and your value systems.

Sex is too good to mess up. Sex without guilt is an absolute must if you are going to find the joy, health and balance you so richly deserve.

9

The Nature of Homosexuality

Gay and lesbian people have chosen their lifestyles for many reasons or motivations. That lifestyle is clearly defined as male loving male, and female loving female, with or without sexual overtones, expressed, or unexpressed. The love expressed may be a genuine unconditional love of the soul, or it can be the sticky, holding possessive love of a jealous and insecure personality. The same applies to heterosexual love.

Gay and lesbian people live together, dance together, play together, suffer together, or live an exciting and wonderful life just the same as heterosexuals do! All lesbians and gays are doing what comes naturally.

Gays and lesbians are just as human, just as loving, caring and sharing as heterosexual couples are with each other. They simply prefer to be sexually active with those of their own gender. They are just as loved and cherished by the source of all that is as those individuals who prefer heterosexual partners of the opposite gender.

If you are gay, lesbian, or bisexual you will understand thoroughly why this is your innately preferred lifestyle. You are normal and not perverted as heterosexual society would have you believe.

If you are lesbian or gay—be what you are with dignity and self-worth. If so, the soul mate that you are yearning for will also possess those same divine characteristics. Love who and what you are!

Man with man and woman with woman, it sounds almost like a song. If it is a song, it grows more popular each and every day. The world is changing and many people are more open about being gay or lesbian, and are more comfortable being in the world as a "couple."

Times have changed dramatically. There are many good reasons for this. A very comprehensive and detailed explanation of how and why this is occurring will be presented shortly. We are merely setting the stage or taking a look at the "play" that is now going on.

Homosexuality stems from natural "drives" or chemical body "triggers." Rather than being unnatural, gay or lesbian individuals are following very natural internal and external promptings. A man loves a man, or a woman loves a woman, and can only find true sexual fulfillment with someone of the same gender because of natural causes!

Basically, many different "mechanisms" are at the root of homosexuality. At conception the incoming entity has up to two weeks to decide whether to be male or female. The determining factor of whether the incoming entity will be male or female does not occur at the conception! Both sex organs are already growing equally in the embryo during those first fourteen days time.

Incidentally, it is the incoming entity that "arranges" the union of the male and female and the conception.

If at the point of conception the entity *chooses* to be a female, the X and Y chromosomes created when the sperm and egg meet sets "the machinery" in motion for a female birth. At the end of 14 to 17 days, if the incoming entity has not changed its mind, the female organ grows and the male organ atrophies. All systems are then set on "forward" to play out the drama of a female birth.

However, if the entity changes its mind and decides somewhere during the two week interval to be born a male instead of a female, that choice is engineered and a male infant will be born. This switch after the initial X and Y chromosome point of conception sets up a great and ongoing hormonal imbalance in that male body, and this imbalance lasts through his entire lifetime. What was originally chosen, designed, and intended to be a female body is now a male vehicle instead! If you haven't noticed, the machinery of a male vehicle is different than the machinery of a female vehicle. This same scenario in reverse could take place if the incoming entity had full intent to be incarnated as a male, then switched to become a female instead.

Another factor is that accidents can and do happen. Suppose the incoming being chooses to become a male, however the X and Y chromosome encounter between the egg and sperm accidently triggers a female conception. If that occurs, the entity being birthed can simply override that train of events anytime during those first fourteen to seventeen days after conception.

In both of these scenarios the final outcome is the same, either a male is birthed into a body that was designed originally to run off of estrogen and progesterone—but now, instead, runs off of testosterone; or a female is birthed into a body that was designed originally to run off of testosterone—but now runs off of estrogen and progesterone. This wreaks havoc both physically and psychologically in the switched bodies. A child becomes a youth that grows up to be a man in what was originally designed to be a female body, or a child grows into a young maiden and then a woman in what was originally designed to be a male body.

This switch after conception is one of the major factors that promotes and underlies homosexuality as a chosen lifestyle.

There can be a host of other factors contributing toward the production of a homosexual rather than a heterosexual posture of living.

The "intent packet" of the parents can contribute strongly toward motivating a homosexual lifestyle. Let us examine the *intent* of both parents—for that intent is always imbedded in both the sperm and the egg. The intent packet of the father goes into the sperm at the point or time of conception and is indelibly imprinted in the DNA and genes of the forthcoming child. The mother's intent packet goes into the DNA and genes of the child through her egg at conception. However, her imprinting of the DNA and genes of the child continues through the entire pregnancy until the birth cord is finally cut.

If, for example, the mother has fantasies about making passionate love to a lot of different men—that attitude is branded into the DNA and genes of the infant—whether it is male or female—to want to grow up and make love to a lot of males. If the infant is male then he will grow up and will want to make love to a lot of men! It's natural for it is in his genes. His homosexual preference is innate and natural to the chemistry of his body.

This identical pattern applies in reverse. If the father fantasizes making love to a lot of women, he implants that tendency into the infant through his sperm. If the infant is female, she will grow up wanting to make love to a lot of females. Her own lesbian preference is natural to the chemistry of her precious body.

Both of these highly emotional intent packets generated through the mother and father are implanted in the fetus. Whatever these factors are can be a contributing reason why the "chemical equation" produces a homosexual individual as the child grows into adulthood.

Sometimes entities are in too great a rush to reincarnate. They come into incarnation too fast, before working out the load of guilts garnered from the last or closest incarnation.

If the entity was a male in that last existence or in the majority of its incarnations, and really loves and enjoys that maleness, the intent at conception will be to be born a male. However, if he accidently winds up in a female embodiment, you have another strong set of circumstances that predetermine sexual preferences. You have a predominantly male entity in a female body that naturally is attracted to females. This same set of circumstances in reverse could put a female in a male body and naturally loving men. Often this is the major reason that a person may feel strongly that he or she is in the wrong body—it's true!

The most dominant factor that makes up our male or our female composite is the "repulsive principle" ratio innate within each one of us. Both polarities of attraction/repulsion contribute to make each one of us uniquely different in our wave vibration and accentuates either a male or a female human expression.

When each one of us individuated, fragmented, or birthed *self* from the "all thing" or the "no thing"—depending on your outlook (or in-look), we had only two generic classes and choices for our "original birth"—male or female.

There are many other realities where a half dozen or a whole dozen of generic classes, or polarity choices, of self birth are possible. All of these polarities are lodged or contained within one physical body. In our reality, only two polarities can be held in the body, male and female.

At this original birth (because of all of the factors of time/space) you were designed to be somewhat equally male/female, or dominantly male, or dominantly female. The ideal in this original design was for male to be enjoined with female, and female to be enjoined with male. This is always how body chemistry works best.

However, some of us are not equally balanced, and the male/female expression will have incarnations that are divided unequally. The human body is too immature to contain all of our vibration, but if 65 percent is female and 35 percent is male in expression our male incarnations will be balanced fine, but our female incarnations will be short-changed—only containing 35 percent femininity. In that case, our female portion of self, if it has incarnated simultaneously in a female body, will feel unfulfilled as a female.

Now in comes another big player in the male/female drama on earth—our second brain. Our second brain, or light brain, keeps track of our many simultaneous male and female lifetimes. It also dispenses the proper flow of male or female hormones into each physical body. If a membrane of the second brain is weak or injured, we can have a bleedthrough from the dominant sexual portion of self in simultaneous incarnation. This means that the second brain can actually change the hormone flow of the body. If a strong second brain bleedthrough of male testosterone comes through, the female with only 35 percent femininity can physically change. The vocal patterns could become quite masculine, the style and walking patterns or body carriage would be more mannish. This gradually produces a lesbian.

This entire pattern can be reversed to apply to the creation of a gay male. All the physics of our "being" are governed strictly by the attraction/repulsion principle. We are mostly all babes learning gradually how to operate these two great and all consuming vital forces within our own natures.

Each one of us is a "face" within the whole entity *self.* In order to "be" and to create our own individual "face" or personality, we had to create a magnetic/repulsive field that enables us to hold ourselves away from the divine source. This repulsion field holds us separate, or apart from the source long enough to build up our own unique identity—which eventually allows us each to become equal to the source—yet as a separate divine and creative entity.

The individual magnetics of each one of us is different in accord to the space/time repulsion principle that separated each of us from the One Source. In order to build a human body in the earth dimension, we each had to choose initially between possessing or occupying a negatively or a positively charged body. That is what determined our expression in either a female or male human incarnation. Therefore, each one of us "came in" originally in that polarity separation as predominantly a male or a female "player."

To complicate matters, the genetics of these yet quite undeveloped human bodies on earth cannot hold all of our vibrations. This means, for example, that if we are a male entity possessing 65 percent male vibrations and 25 percent female vibrations, 10 percent of our total vibratory nature is lost.

If this same male is accidentally born into a female body, only 25 percent of female vibrations are then being held in that incarnation and she will feel very inadequate as a female, and feel strongly that she is in the wrong gender body. This same ratio can be reversed to apply to a natural female who incarnates in a male body. He then will feel inadequate as a male and will feel strongly he is in the wrong gender body.

Using these exact same examples, if the second brain membrane is thin, and bleedthrough occurs from the original male or female—hormones will be activated and the female in the body will respond to male hormones and naturally will become a lesbian. The male in the body will respond to the bleedthrough of female hormones and will naturally become gay, or more feminine and interested in men.

A main point to remember is that if, at your "original separation," when your own magnetic/repulsive system was initiated, even though you were dominantly a male or a female—if, for example, your ratio of male/female energies were 45/40 percent—with 15 percent not containable—you could function in either a male or female body as a normal male or normal female. However, if one polarity is too pronounced, then the other will be lacking and will naturally take on a gay or lesbian lifestyle.

These are some of the key physical or mechanistic reasons which contribute to a natural homosexual interest. There are also emotional factors that contribute to the whole equation of who and what you are at any given time and space *on earth*.

At an emotional level, many males resent being males and wish they were females instead. Females may also resent being females and wish they were males instead. This emotional repulsion toward their own natural bodies arises from ages or lifetimes of discontent. It does appear that the opposite sex has an easier time of it in life. However, appearances are often deceiving. Both sexes have equally hard times during their awareness and growth in this valuable attraction/repulsion field created for our physical existence. Men only think women have an easier time in life! Women only think men have an easier time in life!

This discontent not only arises from observation and deduction at everyday life levels—it also is generated from our DNA and genes. Many of what may be the dominant ancestors living now in our genes felt exactly the same way. This adds to the equation of why some modern males and females hate their own bodies!

Women in the past were treated worse than slaves. They were possessions to be sold, bartered, and killed, or molested at will. Mothers often killed female babies just to spare them from such a life of suffering. It is no wonder women decided they would rather be men.

Men had to be strong, silent, emotionless, ready to kill or die in war after war. Men had to work the fields in the hot sun or bitter cold to support their wives and children. They were not allowed to feel (or be emotional) for that was a social indication that they were weak and not men. It is no wonder that looking at the seemingly easy, well "kept" lifestyle women seemed to "enjoy" made them envious—and the thought or desire of being a woman became strong as a future reality.

These were and still are the thoughts and feelings of your and my ancestors, and these thoughts are still very much alive within us, activating the chemistry of our physical bodies. That pent-up feeling of repression and resentment is strongly fortified when several successive generations of malcontent ancestors hate being males, or hate being females. All of these various equations tend to promote a tendency of a male to disown his male state of being, and to easier relate to other strongly discontented males—and vice versa. Interestingly, the number of male and female homosexuals is quite evenly balanced.

Another Western Christian cultural standard literally that breeds homosexuality also needs to be considered. Males and females are socially separated to keep them from breeding with each other.

Boys are separated from girls. Boys are told to pal around with boys and girls are told to hang out with girls. Even grown men and women are kept under strict social standards in isolation from each other. If a man goes out with a woman everyone looks to see what is going on there, for it is obviously sexual! All this gender separation leads to a great amount of sexual pressure. Men with men or women with women are then eventually going to seek relief or sexual release with their own gender.

That overt separation of the sexes is especially repressive at puberty, when the absolute pinnacle of sexual curiosity and the desire to explore sex occurs. Instead, boys are urged to have male companions and girls are told to find companionship with other girls. The young are taught to mingle and communicate only with their own gender!

Girls do share their feelings and talk with each freely and often become good friends. However, boys do not share feelings—that is considered feminine—they do "masculine" things, like playing baseball and being active together at something. Their friendships are based more on common interests so communicational skills are often lacking. Neither gender learns how to communicate to each other, or how to be best friends with each other. This explains why adult men and women suddenly brought together, or even after long marriages, are unable to communicate with each other. They never learned how to talk with and understand each other in their development. Instead, they were separated and told to avoid the opposite gender. The implication (like in breeding animals) is that the only time males and females are brought together is to reproduce. We were never taught to be women and men who can be friendly with and have great times together. Only a rare few of us ever learn that—and it is usually done on our own.

Though all life is simple, we human beings make it quite intricate. There is no simple singular reason why some of us in human form are homosexual, bisexual, or heterosexual. There is no right or wrong to these different sexual postures. The key point presented here is, that contrary to public thought and education or religion, homosexuality is natural. A homosexual is a divine human being like anyone else and deserves respect and honor.

10

Nature Holds All the Answers

There is no question that nature cannot answer. We need to look again for our answers because the "accepted" schools of thought cannot be trusted, since religion, philosophy, science, and psychology are often not now what they started out to teach. People are also so ready to believe the "statistical truth" of today's media hype that even if the very exact opposite of truth is foisted upon them, it will be consumed without thought.

This tampering has been going on for many centuries. In our churches, great truths (like the philosophy of reincarnation) have been "forgotten" and countless half-truths and outright falsifications of the original pronouncements or prophecies have been skillfully made. These deliberate changes or omissions of truth were made to serve one purpose—to control the gullible masses.

As science developed and psychology was understood, it was swiftly seized, altered, and used to serve the needs of the elite. Brainwashing, or mind control, or control of the media has almost completely lulled everyone to sleep—while homes, businesses, and constitutional rights and freedoms have been robbed, and many don't even know why they think the way they do.

Because homosexuals do not conform to what a dominant heterosexual society wants them to do, they are often condemned and dishonored, and that is totally wrong. One of the arguments used by heterosexuals is that homosexuality is not found in nature—

that animals do not practice homosexuality. The other argument is that sex is only for reproduction of the species. That little "gem" came from the long controlling arm of religion. It was of great benefit for the church and the state for their people to reproduce like rabbits, for making babies brings in more people to the church, and also brings more tithes and taxes. Homosexuality has always been officially denounced by church and state for that very reason, yet both church and "state" knew that homosexuality was practiced by many.

All species have a natural capability to reproduce their own kind. Without such a safeguard the species would soon be extinct. Reproduction of the species is the foremost characteristic of any form of life in the entire universe. Nothing can stop it. We seldom realize that gay and lesbian people have parents. We also don't realize that it's not necessary for every male and female to reproduce. So different lifestyles are not "wrong" as soon as we take the lifestyle of making babies away from our social structure.

Mother Nature has had eternities beyond measure to experiment and discover the most efficient and life fulfilling perpetuation of any species. All "secrets" can be wrested from nature through the technique called decentration—the exact opposite of concentration. Another way to look at this is from the viewpoint of expansion versus compression. When you or I have a question about anything in the universe, from intimate personal matters to the most complex scientific "problem," the solution can always be found through a strong and prolonged opening or expanding of self to the answer within nature.

This is not to be confused with meditation as normally defined. That usually only relaxes the self and rests the mind and body—which is quite healthy but decentration is a more active stance or posture of being. It is dynamic, for you are opening up with deliberate intent to receive. If you realize that the "answer" wants to be "grabbed" as much as you want to grab and hold it within yourself, the process will be empowered greatly.

If you want to find a unique answer that is specific to you, then this technique of decentration could be invaluable. If you remember that what you do or do not do is completely between you and your source, your enlightenment will come speedily. Do not ask your best friend, lover, family or anyone else for advice—the answer stands solely between you and your Maker. None of these others—even though some may be well-intentioned—have the whole, true answer that you may be wanting to know. Trust your nature!

It might help here to repeat that it is not what you take that counts—it is what you give. The self-seeking "takers" will soon be but a memory in planetary evolution, while the freely giving souls will be uplifted and blessed with an abundance beyond the range of human mind to envision.

11

Your Ideal Does Exist

Not only does your most ideal soul mate exist, but so does every ideal conceived by humanity. Every single unique ideal has genuine reality. Each one of us progresses forward into more mature or expanded states of being as we move from ideal to ideal.

As a child, your ideal of being a kindergarten student or graduate became your reality. Then your ideal of middle school, high school, and college followed. Of course, not everyone followed that train of ideals, for some of us branched off into other life paths.

In creation the end is always seen from the beginning! First, you have a vision or insight into your attainment or aspiring goal. Then you are drawn toward them as soon as they become "visible" in your consciousness. Clarity or visibility is the key toward manifestation of any ideal. Your manifestation cannot exceed your clarity about it. You must see and feel it as vividly and intensely as possible.

Your creative thrust follows a threefold step of unfoldment, from idea, to ideal, to idol! You move from the idea, which is something more grand or greater, to the ideal form, shape, or reality of it, to the final realization or materialization of that newly accepted ideal—as a tangible reality, or idol.

You can look back into your own evolving life and you will see how your ideals have pulled and pushed you beyond your apparent talents or abilities.

Once your ideal is achieved or loved into existence, it becomes an idol, or a permanent part of your vast persona or identity. At each new elevation or stage of your life, other new ideas and vistas form new ideals that lure and attract you ever onward, inward and upward!

The cardinal rule is that if it can be imagined it exists!

The very moment you personally focus very strongly upon the aspects and attributes of your ideal soul mate, his or her reality starts to be assured in your life. It is only a matter of time for him or her to materialize into your physical reality. With practice, you can learn how to be an *instant* "thought-do" and "thought-be" creator. The previous "time lag" between your creative thought, desire, action, and physical materialization will disappear. Your creations become instantly real!

You may have noted that you conjure up different aspects or attributes to the form of your ideal mate at different times in your life. Your "choice" looks and personality traits of your ideal mate do change—as you change. As you become more of self, you want an *equal* who can be as much of his or her self as you are now.

To feel worthy of a worthy soul mate who is attractive to you, you must first realize your own genuine worthiness! You must feel and realize your own attractive qualities. That is why "taking charge of your life" and loving your body, while building a good self-image, prepares you for your soul mate encounter.

Only too often in life we "bargain" for a dollar when we are worth a million, meaning you are worth so many times more than what you sell yourself for!

Take the time to feel for and accept your real divine value as you go "shopping" for your ideal soul mate. Give yourself a gift of the greatest love imaginable—and in the most attractively wrapped "package" that *you* can imagine! You alone are the great and grand architect that can design how, why, when and who enters your lifestream of conscious physical reality.

Your soul mate is your ideal and mirrors or reflects the most inspirational qualities that you know in yourself—that your mind and soul can conceive. If you can imagine it, it is in you! He or she is the most adorable lover, friend and spiritual companion you can ever imagine being in your life reality—and be well assured—*he or she does exist*!

Two men come together or two women come together into a soul mate union for the same reason that heterosexuals unite. The soul's learning process is amplified because of relationships. Both body and soul gain wisdom and greater depths of dimension and self-awareness when you find and build harmonic relationships with another "light being" in human body.

A soul mate union also allows your physical body to know and thrill to the human physical touch and love experienced through physical contact with a mate who vibrates at the same comfortable soul frequency level as yourself, sexually and sensually, like no other human experience can ever do! Whether you are gay or lesbian, nature, as explained throughout this text, has brought you and your ideal partner together to further develop your feelings of self-worth and greater self-spirituality. Simply be who and what you are with dignity and genuine self-love.

12

Improving Your Self-Image

Your possession of a good self-image is tremendously important. Unless your self-image will allow it, the possibility of materializing a soul mate in your life is zero! Your image of you controls your health, it controls your wealth, it controls your love life, and it controls the myriad of daily events you experience during entire human existence.

Think it through! If you love yourself your daily life will be flooded with loving events. If you hate yourself, your daily life will be filled with hateful events.

Only a rare few self-realized individuals on earth today truly know and love who and what they are. That rarity occurs because you and I, and all humanity, are born into a society immersed in strong feelings and false convictions of guilt. That sea of guilt at the surface of the planet is further amplified through our genetic codes and DNA. Our additional burdens of lack, ignorance, and a host of other negative living conditions further expand our thoughts and feelings of self-depreciation and self-guilt.

Check it out. If you are loaded with feelings of self-guilt, doubts, regrets and other signs of self-depreciation you simply cannot find room for love of self. Without that genuine appreciation and high regard for your own thoughts and feelings, or actions, a good self-image will be impossible to build and hold.

How does anyone—you specifically—break out of this ongoing self-destructive guilt atmosphere long enough to find self and rebuild your heavy laden self-image? The answer is only through knowledge. Knowledge alone can set you free! When, through knowledge, you realize your true divinity and self-worth, you will stop hating yourself, or things about yourself, and you will eventually break away from that vicious cycle of guilt after guilt surrounding you at every turn of your life.

You can learn to improve your self-image by consciously and deliberately thinking, feeling, doing, loving and appreciative things for yourself and others. Instead of being critical, look for and find the very highest and best of everything inside of your own being and inside of others. Be quick to note and express real thankfulness for the beauty and abundance surrounding you, and expressed from within yourself and others.

You may have to begin with an "act as if" attitude for a while, but you cannot fake it. Your thoughts and feelings must be really you.

You can only love you if you are lovable. Again, what makes you lovable? Thinking and expressing lovable thoughts and actions toward yourself and others! When you look and finally see your self-worth your new self-image will reflect your new radiance. Your world will change as old "friends" will disappear and new friends more like the new you appear.

At that point you are already very electric and highly magnetic. When your self-image is good you feel *safe*, your ego is no longer needed for defense. You are comfortable with meeting your "equal"—your soul mate—who now also possesses a great self-image, for he or she must be a mirror image of you!

Another important key to elevating your self-image is through moving out of self-ignorance through conscious self-education. Have fun learning about *you* and the grand universe that fills your existence with such great abundance. Learn the simple universal laws that brought you out of nothing and into this incredible world of endless existence.

A knowledgeable person is always self-confident and prone to display an admirable and commanding self-image. Give yourself a constant craving or thirst for knowledge. That is a superb gift of pure love to yourself! Knowledge will never hurt you. It will often dispense seeming pain at will. Your knowledge brings light into the dark part of *your* world—and a socially darkened world—where you can be a light.

Turn off that horrendous, mind-controlling TV and that abominable radio "music." Stop attending violent, desensitizing movies and read a good informational nonfiction book—or something light.

Security of your identity or self-image comes through self-knowledge *only*. When you feel safe, your ego is no longer threatened, and you will begin to communicate your peace, your joy, and your love to your life companions—and to your soul mate—to be re-given back to you!

A good self-image is always attractive. It draws others into your aura, while a "bad" self-image is just as equally repulsive, and others will avoid your presence.

In that light, I hope by the time you have finished reading this book you will have taken charge of your good life and will begin to drop all of your guilts, your self-regrets, and your "I should haves" out of your daily expression. Leave them in the past, where they belong, with your ancestors as events already lived. What you claim, you own! Make every regret a pearl of wisdom instead. Go *forward*, not backward, knowing *you are infinitely more than your body* and any past event. Acknowledge the god that is within you and your new self-image will be strong, everlasting and mighty beautiful!

Pretend that you hear someone repeatedly asking you the question, "Who are you?"

Now answer that question. Each time you answer it, think, feel, ponder and go deeper and deeper for the honest answer. After going six or seven "levels" deep your persistent search will encounter that feeling of sure strength—an absoluteness—that is you! You will feel like the Rock of Gibraltar. Nothing can move you from your center of balanced expression. Your new self-image is now alive and well.

13

The Power of True Prayer

True prayer is not a bleating plea to GOD for worldly or unworldly desires. It has nothing to do with the fine or gross words spoken by mind or mouth. Prayer of that nature is never answered, heard, or fulfilled by the source, or GOD—as the *source* is defined by religion.

Only true active prayer has the power to fulfill your desire, whether you are praying for mundane things, or for a soul mate, or for any other dynamic life or death desires! If it is not wishful thinking or incessant begging to our greater source—for fulfillment of our desires—what is true prayer?

True prayer begins as thought and personal feelings followed by action toward formation of your desire. As survival or material desire arises within you and is strong enough to move you toward inspired action, your prayer is true and begins movement toward formation and physical materialization.

A prime example of true prayer is when a farmer wants a crop of corn, all his actionless pleadings and ceaseless begging for GOD to send him a crop of corn will not produce it. However, when the wise farmer wants a crop of corn, he prepares the soil, plants the virile seed (no hybrid, please), then lovingly nourishes and waters the fledgling corn plants. His sustained desire and true prayer of action toward bringing in a good crop of corn becomes a reality. Nature, or the source fulfilled that prayer unhesitatingly.

Words by themselves, without action, lack true power and the feeling power or electrical intensity needed to summon the universal thrust needed to make the wanted desire. The first requirement of true prayer, like in all creative action, is to know what you truly want! Then increase the clarity and the focus, with intense feeling and appropriate action.

Many of our lives are like a series of false prayers lacking clarity and correct action. Waking up to the art of true prayer will cure that. My prayer is that the information I have presented to you will aid you in finding your soul mate. I followed that desire and went into action to present this knowledge to you—the rest is up to you!

14

The Dynamics of Self-Suggestion

The technique of finding your soul mate, like any effective technique, works, but only if you work it! Self-suggestion plays one of the major factors in the bringing of your own body into attunement, in range with your soul mate. It will not matter where on earth he or she may be. Self-suggestion literally charges up the body and electrically creates the strong magnetic field you need to focus in and draw your soul mate to you.

No matter what it is that you desire to materialize in your physical reality, self-suggestion will help you to speed up the process immensely. In most successful techniques, self-suggestion, or self-hypnosis is the most overlooked and underrated, yet the most effective "tool" available to strengthen and reinforce your focus and resultant success.

Focus automatically aids clarity and intensifies your electrical potential. Your desire acts like a strong magnet, if that desire is sufficiently focused and highly charged. When any thought is strongly felt, its dynamic potential and magnetism increases proportionately.

If you do not already own some good books or audiotapes on learning self-hypnosis, I suggest you go to your nearest bookstore and acquire some. Hundreds have been published and many are very well written by competent and knowing practitioners, often doctors, psychologists, or psychiatrists.

Do not let any less informed or well-meaning, but ignorant friend or advisor tell you that hypnosis or self-suggestion is dangerous or "bad" for you. There has never been a single documented case of anyone ever harming themselves, while millions of individuals have achieved great health and success with it—people from all walks and positions in life!

Essentially, self-suggestion is simply a matter of taking or making some "quiet time" and putting all of the feeling you can muster into the thought—in this case—that you are ready for your soul mate to arrive physically in your life. This charges up every cell of your body and sends out a powerful signal to the cells in the body of your soul mate—announcing that you are physically around, ready, and available—and summons him or her to you. That signal encompasses all earth, so your soul mate could be in a foreign country and yet would get the call. My soul mate did!

Once that initial rapport is firmly established, it is then only a matter of time before the two of you will wend your way, step by step, to each other. He or she could suddenly decide for no apparent reason to visit your area. Your two lines of magnetic pulsation and attraction will meet. When that physical encounter occurs you will know it! Sparks will fly! The knowingness or powerful feeling that you have known each other for ages is true. The indelible memory of his or her vibration or wave length is in your DNA and genes.

When impact occurs, the two of you will blast or ease your way into a flow that re-ignites and reunites the passionate and deep love known in your body cells by your ancestors before. That grand past love is now alive and enhanced by your own "new love." It will also be a great heritage of love that you will pass along up through the genes of your children and their children's children, ad infinitum.

Self-suggestion becomes greatly empowered through the force of repetition. That repetition imbeds your idea or thought-form with more life—every time you think or feel it!

You are not limited to your practice during quiet times. You can vitalize and recharge your persistent desire any time of the night or day, while driving your car, taking out the garbage, or performing other such mundane tasks that require little conscious attention.

In this wonderful art of self-suggestion the normal conscious aware mind must be bypassed. You need to get past it into the subconscious mind that holds you a prisoner to your present situation. It has been proven again and again that in a contest between the conscious mind and the subconscious, the subconscious always wins the battle. This happens because your subconscious is loaded with doubts, guilts, fears, and "I can't" attitudes that are deeply engrained into your cellular being. Proper techniques utilizing self-suggestion allow you to bypass your conscious mind and rewrite the new message into your subconscious.

Wise individuals use all of the tools available to insure success. Take time to formulate a short, but powerful phrase, seven words or less, that communicates or sends the message of what you desire. This helps to put it into the subconscious so it can be transmitted from your cellular being to his or her cellular being. That message can be beamed out to your soul mate at least three times every day. For example: "Please come to me! I love you!"

Make it your thought and your message from your own unique essence, so formulate the message you send to your "special someone" in your choice of images and feelings. Your greatest power is generated when you are 100 percent yourself! Use self-suggestion to achieve any goal that you wish. It can play a key factor in attracting your soul mate into your life.

15

How Safe Is Your Love?

How safe is your love? This is a seemingly odd question. However, from the standpoint of discovering exactly who and what you are, this may be the most important chapter in this book!

You may think you have your own thoughts and feelings, but the truth is that your body chemistry evokes your thoughts and feelings at least 98 percent of the time. You are more a pawn of fate than the ruler of your destiny. You are living off the past.

Knowing self may sound easy, for you can think and say, "I know me. I am an artist, I am a computer operator, I am a salesperson, or I am one or more of a billion structures."

You assume that you are your name, or your body, or your vocation, or whatever. You believe all these images you cling to hold your identity.

No structure or limited form of any kind could ever constitute or hold all of your great unknown identity! You are beyond containment of any cellular or organic limitation of body, beyond any mentally-walled prison of self-identity.

You are and always will be formless and forever alive! That should be good news to you. No matter how many different "coats of skin" you put on or take off—in all your infinite dimensions of reality—they are all relative illusions—in each relative dimension or plane.

Normally, the closest you can come to your identity of self is through your feeling of sure strength, of absolute security, and the feeling of infinite calm. That is your absolute zero universal position in time/space out of which all of your thought, power and presence arises. That is you!

Your layers of self-images do not reveal you, they conceal you! The fastest way to disrobe the layer upon layer of ephemeral and grossly false self-identity—unveiling your true immortal self—is to find absolute safety in your every world interaction or involvement. This is also a relatively easy and expedient path to awareness of your *whole* self. (That other self is the unholy one!)

To begin, get a large sheet of paper and compile two self-revealing lists in writing. One is your "safe" list and the other is your "unsafe" list. Now go to work. Begin listing all the things that make you feel safe or unsafe. To do it right you should have well over a hundred "things" listed on each list. Evaluate things, events, possibilities and probabilities that are relative to you. At first the list of safe things may seem a lot easier to fill, but when you find deeper levels, you are most likely to learn there is some subtle connotation of unsafety somewhere. Keep on scanning your world and ask the question of safety.

For example: "Is sex safe, is my job safe, is love safe, is friendship safe, is money safe, is nature safe, is smoking safe, is alcohol safe, is doing drugs safe, is fire safe, is the dark safe, is daytime safe, is togetherness safe, is isolation safe, is a large crowd safe, is TV safe, is radio safe, is a nuclear society safe, is electricity safe, is a characterless society safe, is a governed society safe, is a free society safe, is total freedom safe, etc."

When making your lists you must be 100 percent honest with yourself, otherwise this life-giving technique will not work! Additionally, you may find yourself plumbing several depths or levels of your subject or object. That indicates great progress.

For example: you may at first write down that total freedom is safe. You place it quickly on your list. However, if you probe deeper you may feel quite unsafe about total freedom. Total freedom means that no one need care for you. You do not need to care for another object or being, including your lover, parents, friends, home, money, etc. Are you totally ready for that formless and unlimited freedom?

Most of us in human form make the choice as we have done in countless lifetimes to practice "limited" freedom! We want or need to feel validation through a lover or friend, through a parent or child, through a home or a car, through job, country, tradition, etc. We maintain a safe and respectable distance from total freedom, while flirting with illusions of self-freedom.

Total self or whole self means pure unlimitedness from shape, form or structure in any way! It means being anything or everything at will, effortlessly. It means being nothing (no thing) materially—but everything potentially! As long as your identity depends on any kind of form or structure, it remains vulnerable and unsafe. Even the simple thought, "I am," forms an image and limited identity.

When you chart correctly what is presently safe or unsafe, your true psychology becomes known to you alone. You will discover that if you take each unsafe item listed, one by one, and go deeply, level after level, you will find calmness, security, joy, and strength underneath that mental form or physical structure. When your entire unsafe list is listed, understood (stood-under) and defused from fear, you will be safe and you will know self totally!

Each unsafe item unloaded off of your back will ease your daily burden as your load lightens. You will definitely feel lighter and lighter, brighter and brighter, as the thick smothering layers of illusion (maya) are peeled away from your present very illusory identity. You may choose to remain limited, dependent upon, and controlled by your body chemistry and genes. However, if you do, it will now be your conscious choice and you will find it difficult to play the victim role very convincingly anymore. After all, you know you chose your position. It would be like the rich young man donning beggar clothes, dirtying his face and body and living with the beggars as one of them—just to "lower" himself and understand them. His game is flawed. He can never understand them, for they are destitute, and he is not. Underneath that clever guise as a beggar he knows full well his richness and physical security. He fools only the beggars, but himself more—as long as he plays the beggar game, no matter how earnestly he plays the game! I know a rich young man who plays that game.

Give thanks, for you now have a golden key in your own hands that unlocks all doors and leads to infinite self-expression and god-consciousness—beyond any of your sweetest and wildest dreams.

"To be, or not to be" can now be understood in a whole new light. The paradox of "not to be" allows you total freedom and full control over everything!

As long as you hold your identity in any kind of a structure you are vulnerable, except of course, when the whole you (the complete you) deliberately and knowingly chooses to momentarily occupy any given thoughtform or physical "reality" form. While you are still in the school of human attraction/repulsion education, any ego or identity creates limitation of self and complete freedom, and brings pain.

Please note that while working at overcoming anything on your unsafe list, it is not enough to think and say—for example: "Sex is safe!" You must sincerely feel that sex is safe, or whatever object or subject is safe. Only the deep feeling of security signals the truth that sets you free!

When all vestiges of dark fear are gone and you know the genuine joy, calmness, security and strength beneath any of your unsafe items, go on to delete the next, and the next, until no more unsafe life experiences or expressions exist anymore for you. From that point on, not only do you truly know yourself, you are now forever unlimited. There can never be any bounds, bonds, or limits to your self-expression anywhere and anytime again in the entire known universe—which aptly now constitutes your full or whole self-identity.

16

The Chromosome #23 Factor

Give or take a few thousand years either way, about 70,000 years ago, each and every human body on earth was normal and fully operational on twenty-two chromosomes. "It" was also equally male/female in one healthy human form—which lived on and on. When Chromosome #23 was added, it split that species into what is obviously now distinctly separate male and female bodies. The combination of Chromosome #23 and Chromosome #14 also released the virus we call death, for the first time, for the human body. Prior to that each dual-sexed entity simply self-cloned when a new body form was desired.

Chromosome #23 polarized the human body into either male or female form. In the male body the uterus and breasts would not develop, and in the female body the male genitals would not develop.

This incredible leap, or side-step, in evolution forced each now separate unit of the human species to mate with its opposite gender in order to continue the procreation of the species. The attraction/repulsion principle literally eternalized in the human physical body.

Whereas prior to that epoch-making event, each dual-sexed entity in human form was complete and self-reliant, as well as totally self-fulfilled—now a strong physical and psychological need for togetherness was vitally essential and quickly established. Males were hormonally attracted to females, and females were now hormonally attracted to males, assuring that new generations would be issued and thus the continuance of our human species.

During that long period of time when our human species was asexual, the female trait of gentleness was a predominant characteristic of our human race. At the same time, an asexual entity had full self-expression of power over life, birth and rebirth. That is in stark contrast to our modern civilization where dependency on "other than self" has been instilled and inbred for the past five hundred years—in order that we would become dependent upon the "powers that be" that run civilization today and mold social consciousness. The self-reliant individual has almost become extinct!

One of the explanations for bisexual lifestyles can probably be traced back through the genes when all of us performed sexually as a male or female in our asexual bodies. So bisexuality also stems from natural expressions of human life on earth.*

---

* More data on Chromosome #23 is available from Homewords, Box 57396, Salt Lake City, UT 84157. Telephone (801) 265-9272 (*The Phillip Material*).

17

The Psychology of Homosexuality

The fact I taught an accredited course in psychology at the University of Humanistic Studies, San Diego campus, may add credibility to my presentation of this chapter, so I will mention it.

One of the biggest "crimes" on earth today is our sexuality! Humans are punished more for sexuality than any violent criminal act. A gay or lesbian individual is especially socially ostracized because he or she has the nerve to "do it" with their own sex!

The great psychological question here, since psychology is the science of mind and behavior, is whether or not homosexuality is natural human behavior. The answer without equivocation is a resounding, yes, yes, yes! Our psychological attitudes and actions spring from our physical and spiritual nature. The deep sexual "drives" and behavioral tendencies are all clearly encoded in our DNA and genes and are all natural self expressions. That includes any proclivity toward a homosexual life style, as well. Any moral condemnation of homosexuality is wrong! It is out of place, out of touch, close-minded and ignorant criticism, and is often the result of programming from the church.

What exactly is a homosexual? Is he or she a sexual deviant and someone to be scorned and shunned? That depends on who is doing the talking! However, from a purely objective psychological viewpoint, of course not! A homosexual is exactly like every other human being on earth. He or she goes through all the life lessons, the drama of joy, suffering, pain and ecstasy, like all of us in the human family.

A homosexual is just as human, just as respectable and divine, and deserves to be treated with honor and dignity, just as we treat people with honor and dignity when they have heterosexual preferences! Being different is no crime. It is actually one of the other major outcomes of the introduction of *Chromosome #23* into our genetic pool. Prior to that everyone was pretty much look-alikes and act-alikes. Now we are taller, shorter, heavier, lighter, blondes, redheads, brunettes, blue-eyed, brown-eyed, green-eyed, etc., and I consider that to be a great leap in evolution that will improve our species. Being different is a great compliment, not a put-down, in my book! Besides, allowing others to be themselves and to do their "own thing" is a spiritual attitude. Gay and lesbian people are here on earth to learn human life lessons like everyone else.

The modern homosexual usually processes a great amount of psychological pain in the pursuit of his or her life expressions or repressions. Basically, all that pain stems from feeling disconnected from the body. It is almost always a *separation* issue. As a homosexual you are "different," "do not fit in," "not understood," and are generally ostracized from public acceptance.

Society is determined that the only "cure" for homosexuality is to turn homosexuals "back" into heterosexuals. That way everyone has the same issues! This is a cause of great pain to every homosexual being—for they are naturally what and who they are! They can't help being what they are and are mostly at a loss to cope with such a gross social misunderstanding.

In addition, many gay and lesbian people are highly sensitive and beautiful natured beings. Many of our very finest, upstanding, outstanding and grand world citizens of today are homosexual. They were in our past history, and they will be in our future.

The homosexuals who publicly admit their homosexuality are bold and courageous pioneers. They are not afraid to make the public statement, "*I am different*!" To bravely acknowledge that truth is the biggest issue any gay individual will encounter. That is obviously an issue of separation. The intrepid homosexual making that statement publicly is sounding the broadcast to stop all forms of public isolation that separates homosexuals from society. They are not separate!

Homosexuals, like heterosexuals, have chosen their life style to learn their human lessons in the attraction/repulsion principle on earth. The lesson is, however, not to focus on the pain, on the strangeness, on the differences, on their homosexuality. Instead, the focus needs to be, "I know I am different, and it is all right! The public may ostracize me, but I will not ostracize myself! Within myself, I like who and what I am! Within myself, I choose it! Within myself, I love what and who I am! Within myself, I have grown a lot because of it!"

This is called the face, embrace and erase spiritual technique, and is needed to clarify self by both homosexuals and heterosexuals. It works! However, a word of caution; this inner statement must not be expressed as a hurting and defensive ego defense posture, a rebellious "I don't care" attitude. That is only the same old tango! Instead, your statement must come sincerely from your heart and soul. It is your inner awakening of your love, understanding, and your allowance of self to really be who and what you have chosen to be!!

When the homosexual community learns to be at peace, to be comfortable with who and what they are, they will cease to be considered fearfully odd and strange and ostracized. It takes a new perspective to bring about a new paradigm shift. When this shift to consciousness is implemented by a majority of homosexuals, they will simply be acknowledged as different and allowed that difference socially again, as they were in the days of the Roman empire.

Everyone in human form on earth is loved and worth being loved! That is the greatest and final lesson of life on earth now. Everyone is worth being loved and respected. You are being loved, honored and respected, whether you realize it, or not! When you can realize and accept that, it does not matter what your sexual preferences are, and you can find a partner who can fulfill your partnership needs in a deep and enduring way.

18

The Nature of Heterosexuality

Sex is one of the best, if not *the* best, experiences on earth! Yet because of religious and political desire to control people, sex is the most repressed and potentially explosive human energy on our planet. Even hardened felons are considered in a better light than sexual "offenders." Of course that word is prejudiced, offend what, offend who?

Many insist heterosexuals constitute the mass or bulk of sexual taste or interaction, they insist that everyone who does not conform to their lifestyle is offensive and subject to suspicion and fear. This just happens to be the nature and stage of "the animal" at this point. Of course, most human beings are more than animals, for all of us in human form are more than our bodies.

Civilization on earth is ruled by heterosexual attitudes and beliefs. If you are bisexual or homosexual you threaten this present civilization, for it is weak and fearful. That weakened condition is the accumulation of centuries of teaching and demanding that individuals give up self-reliance and self-sufficiency and become dependent on a group, be it political or religious.

Sex is the most driving human force, so if you can succeed in controlling, inhibiting or repressing sex, you can control the individual and how he or she expresses. The aim is to keep everyone the same! The paradox is that by separating the sexes at an early age and all through their growing life you naturally promote homosexuality. It is like the game of trying not to think of a green turtle, the more you try not to think of it, the more you think of it! Repressed sex is somewhat like that, too. The more you are told not to express or experience it, the more you begin to want to express and experience it, and the more the sensual experience is separated from love. If you are separated with your own gender, then the only other viable option is to express or explore sex with your own gender.

Somewhere along the line, heterosexuals decided that homosexuality was an illness, and that the obvious cure would be to convert them back into heterosexuals again. Of course, the word "convert" gives you a strong idea about the stream of religious/governmental power involved. On the contrary, heterosexuality needs the cure instead! The cure will allow bisexuals, homosexuals, or asexuals their own choice and their own "right of way." Hopefully, that cure will be speeded up if and when enough heterosexuals understand the points presented in this book. They need this cure, so they can go on living their own lives instead of seeking to repress the life styles of others.

19

Where Can I Find My Soul Mate?

"Oh, where is my soul mate?" It sounds almost like a popular song. In fact, I believe it to be the "song of life!" I have heard that question over and over at personal levels or through letters written to me as the author of *Finding Your Soul Mate*.

The answer is that your soul mate is probably never where you think of looking for him or her. I have not yet—out of the many thousands of soul mate couples I have encountered—ever found one single case of a soul mate being found through an intensive physical search, from bar to bar, or dance to dance.

This is because your soul mate is your equal and will like the things you like and will be where you normally spend your waking or sleeping hours. You will find him or her through the fastest and most direct route when you stop looking externally at places or events. Your own unique soul mate will walk, run, or slide into your life when you least expect it. You need to leave a "gap" in your consciousness for her or him to fill. Just as the old saying goes, "many roads lead to Rome." Also, the roads that lead to you stretch and wind clear across the earth. When you have done all of your preparatory work of feeling and being worthy of great love it will come to you. Like is always attracted to like via the inner planes, rather than via outer "surface" roads.

The amount of hours, days, weeks, and years of empty and useless searching for a soul mate externally by lonesome soul mates would boggle your mind. That search is on the wrong dimension. It only leads to endless frustration and empty arms. All genuine connections start between you and your soul mate at consciousness levels. Then the sparks fly and the mental and body signals follow, gently or violently steering the two of you together. All you need to do is hold the focus. It will be worth it!

20

Attitudes of Church, State and Society

The gay or lesbian person stands under attack and suspicion on all major fronts, from church, state, and society. This has been the case in our modern history. Any sexual act or posture contrary to popular heterosexual standards is looked on with downright hostility. However, things appear to be loosening up a little. Even the IRS is opting toward allowing gay "couples" to live together in the USA with tax privileges similar to those held by legal or common-law heterosexual couples.

While government is pushing for gay and lesbian rights, the church on the broad world-wide scale still maintains a strong attitude and position that homosexuality is a "sin." Of course, changes are even coming as a few "new age" ministers and churches allow and welcome gay and lesbian members. Some ministers are openly practicing homosexuality. President Clinton has pledged his full support of the gays to serve in the military. We will see how that goes. Government "rides the fence" while doing what it wants.

Society, slowly being shaped by the elite to fit their goals, has, over the generations allowed drugs, pornography, and wild gang behavior, but still holds the homosexual in fear, and often loathing.

Society may continue to battle against homosexuality, but over the long run, it will lose the battle. The DNA and genes that spark homosexual lifestyles are not about to be erased or changed easily. Society errs when it tries to change a natural lifestyle expressed by a gay or lesbian person into what would be for them an unnatural state of feeling, being and acting. A homosexual is what he or she is—and that is natural! Society, being what it is, is probably going to keep right on trying to pretend homosexuality is not there.

21

The Hidden Causes of Human Behavior

When something is hidden it cannot be visibly seen or confronted. The hidden cause of human behavior is both internally and externally triggered. The inside triggers are at work in the chemistry of our bodies at all times—awake or asleep. Even dreams are channels or outlets for repressed thoughts and feelings from external "sources." You are what you are at any given point in time by what your body communicates to you—and to others. We can only exercise a small amount of control over these hidden causes until we know what they are and how to take back our own powerful control over our lives again. That is why self-knowledge is more important than all of the gold in the world. Gold can inspire "good works" on the "outside" or external world, but is worthless internally! Knowledge, however, can lead you to control over both inner and outer planes of your reality.

When you understand the build-up of your body mass and the simple overlay of genetic coding in your genes and DNA you are well on your way toward self-realization and self-control. When you know why you are homosexual or heterosexual you will be at ease with your chosen lifestyle, not before. You chose it. It is now your lesson. Give thanks that you are naturally what you are.

In a 1993 edition of Contact, a weekly newspaper published in Las Vegas, the author disclosed some of the invasions of human privacy that can occur through the misuse of science. He tells how the Tavistock Institute of Sussex, England has been researching and implementing mind control techniques for the general public. These machines have now been developed to the point that physical drives can be programmed and changed, i.e., causing homosexual (or heterosexual) hormone cessation at the blink of an eye; even personalities can be changed at the blink of a pulse-wave-probe.

Our lives are being shaped and led world-wide today by TV, radio, movies, newspapers, magazines, and books, all owned by a tiny handful of rich families. You are being fed daily what those families and their communication systems want you to know and believe. There is much hidden that they do not want you to know about. If you are asleep and unaware of these awesome hidden currents of activity, they can sweep you away. If, on the other hand, you search out and acquire knowledge about who and what is running or ruining your life, you can step off of the train and go forward toward your own direction again.

Good luck, and watch both ways!

22

Take Charge of Your Life

When you take charge of your daily life, you begin to control your future. The reason becomes obvious when you realize that every tomorrow had its basis in today. Your tomorrow literally grows out of your present moments in this day.

Life is like a giant ocean-wave-camera that takes vivid snapshots of your "today." Each moment is a snapshot that is duly recorded and reproduced on the next wave, forever and ever without end. This means what you think or dwell on today must be recorded and repeated. This insight is a sobering thought. It means you already possess the means and the power to create your tomorrow. It also shows the importance of taking responsibility for your particular focus or perspective of the world. You then are the sole creator of your world and the reality you encounter in it. That is an immutable Universal Law. When you concentrate on your having fun and abundance today, you will be "measured out" an equal amount of fun and abundance tomorrow. When you concentrate on your lack of joy and state of abject poverty or pain, you have set yourself up for more lack of joy, poverty and pain tomorrow! It's your choice! Isn't this game fun?

Now realizing how nature duplicates your every feeling and thought, you can start this moment to keep on generating the kind of feelings, thoughts and life experiences worthy of your image of self!

In the same manner that your creativity cannot exceed your clarity, you cannot accept or allow what your self-image cannot validate. Be careful about what you think and feel. Someone or something special is watching you. The whole universe watches to see and notes, or records, what you are focusing on—so that it can give you more of the same. That watchful source does not ever judge or put any personal evaluation on what you do and what you want. It loves you and will give you back, again and again, what appears to be your desire or focus. You are never a victim, for you accepted or allowed every event of your existence in human form.

When your focus dwells on being with your soul mate, nature will rush to fill in that void. Remember to put your thoughts and feelings on your soul mate being in your life, not the lack of one. Always focus on the solution or answer, not on the problem or question!

I repeat, for great care must be taken here, focus on the fulfillment and presence of your soul mate with you, or whatever else you truly desire in your future.

Your past is already lived and gone forever, and the future is only a stage or screen to reflect, play out, or consume your present desires in the ETERNAL NOW! So sort out and choose carefully which images, desires, thoughts, feelings and actions you "implant" into the present moment. Each one will be recorded and repeated in equal, or greater, or lesser harvest, according to, and in direct ratio to, your thoughtful or unthinking input.

This knowledge of how creation works is to inspire you to take charge of your every precious life moment. When you add appreciation, reverence, life and growth to your consciousness, it returns to you, again and again. You are loving yourself into eternal existence!

On the other hand, if you surrender or give away control of our life moments, then you arrest your growth, and disdain, or lack of the self-respect, death and decay flood or overwhelm your reality.

Life is simple, not complex. When this simple recording and duplicating process is known, as it now is by you, or by any group, or by any civilization, then you, or that group, or that civilization will know how to take charge of the future! Then the rate of evolution, self-growth, self-knowledge, self-control, and self-respect will skyrocket, instead of the existing, struggling snail's pace of enlightened change and development.

Combine this knowledge with the foregoing knowledge—that almost all of your thoughts and feelings arise from your body chemistry, from your ancestral past, and you will know how important it is for you, the present you, to take charge of your life. You can begin to direct your course in life toward your goals, not toward the old goals of your ancestors—or the goal of an external dominant figure your life now!

This knowledge gives you a "window of opportunity" to seize control of your ship (body) and steer for the stars! You always bog down or sink your ship further every time you give away your own unique power of discernment to someone else, or to a religion, or to any of so many limited schools of thought that want to take care of you.

Make your own decisions. Who are you? What are you? Only your answer counts!

In this priceless "now moment" you are whatever you choose to dwell upon, and that is your you of tomorrow. This is how you creatively unfold your future days and nights of forever.

Like every other human being on earth you are faced with a huge challenge. You must eventually learn how to stop running off of the chemistry of your body—by turning the situation around 100 percent, so that your body chemistry is subordinate to you! This means that most of us have a long way to go, not in time, but in achieving mastery over our bodies. At present, most of the neural lights "firings" stem from ancestral mitochondria living in our genes and DNA, from body chemistry, instead of from the bright divine god consciousness of our being—deep within us. It is like stumbling in the dark, instead of walking securely and somewhat arrogantly in the light of a bright sunny day!

Each and every rising moment in your daily consciousness is a golden door to your reality. Fill it to the brim with golden joy, love and abundant life—for what you put in is exactly what you get out in return. Why not then choose love, instead of hate, choose joy instead of sorrow, choose life, instead of death? It's not my choice—it's yours! What do you choose?

23

Loving Your Body

Homosexual, bisexual, heterosexual, so what? Your sexual choice does not matter! But why is it so hard for you to love your body?

The most precious possession you have or will ever have on earth is your body. Without it you are a no thing! You are essentially a fragment or a spark of light. Without your physical body you cannot touch, feel, sense, or express all the emotions and deep feelings you have within your depths of being. Without that magnificent body of yours, you cannot express that great and passionate desire and love you hold for your soul mate.

Your body was designed and created by the gods, including yourself, to become a vehicle worthy of conveying your individual light expression, so that you could see, touch, feel, smell, and taste all of your wonderful creations on earth!

Your first human bodies were not so beautiful and so sensitive when they were first created. All of them looked the same. However, like all living creations in nature they have gradually evolved into being the individually unique and attractive vessels they all are today.

You may not like your body, or actually hate it, but your inner entity self, or god-being, holds great love and thrills of excitement for your body. It will eventually attain immortality and will be carried by you in it to the stars, and through many other subtle and now unknown realms or dimensions of godly existence and godly adventures.

Most of the time, instead of uplifting and aiding our body to achieve its own immortality with us, we abuse it, curse it, and greatly fail to realize what a grand and important gift we have given to ourselves in it. Our bodies are not being loved and appreciated, they are being overfed, underfed, drugged, overworked, underworked, and generally kept in poor condition and disrespect.

Without daily use, the muscles of your body lose tone and wither as old age sets in. You then dislike your body even more for failing you, when you have actually failed it! It has grown old because of your lack of love, your great neglect, and your years of despising it.

Your body is loaded with intelligence. It is not recognized or understood as having an incredible pool of knowledge within it. Yet, each and every single cell of that body of yours contains all the thoughts and all the knowledge of all your ancestors—over twenty billion of them! Each and every single one of your body cells holds enough knowledge within it to rebuild, not only our known universe, if it were ever destroyed, but countless other unknown universes as well. Can you match that?

From a physical standpoint, your body lives in the past. It has been created totally from the past and is only today materializing for you the strong thoughts or desires you may have had five or ten years ago. Your body needs to be lovingly taught how to live in the present—and how to move fluidly into the future with you. That is one of your tasks.

Your body is also quite fearful. It knows that you are supposed to be running or guiding it, while instead you are gone most of the time. You live so much in so many of your past events, or in your near and distant future events that you miss the "now."

In terms of evolution, the organ you know as your body is very young. It is still comparatively a child that keeps struggling so hard to perform as an adult for you. It cannot, for it is not matured like the adult light being "riding within it"—you, your self, a living god!

Your conscious task is to merge your beautiful body and your beautiful spirit into one synchronized god being. At the present, you are vibrating at a much higher frequency than your body. When you are able to bring your biological body and your biological personality to a totally 100 percent pulsation at the same vibratory rate, that separation will be gone for all time. Your body will then be able to shift along with you at the speed of thought into any atomic frequency level. It can go on through the atoms to the moon, or through solid steel walls, simply by shifting into atomic frequencies as quickly as you can shift your thought! That is the big "ideal" and the "end goal" in this grand and fully consummated "marriage" of your body to your spirit!

Just think how wonderful it is. Your own beautiful body contains the entire feeling tone and history of everyone who has ever walked upon or existed on this earth. It is a magnificent creation, but the primitive human brain within it is young. It needs much further development. This is another good reason why the generation of joy is so important to your physical being. The high frequency of joy speeds up body development. It links the entire fourfold brain network: (1) primitive brain, (2) light brain, (3) intellectual brain, and (4) solar plexus brain, into one complete and powerfully operating whole system—merging and bonding your body and spirit into one uninterrupted and unlimited flow.

These two vastly different worlds of body and spirit are now positioning or moving into a "window of opportunity" for a dramatic and blissful merger!

When you truly know that your body is the carriage of the gods, you will treat it more lovingly as the grand possession it is—and always has been to you!

You cannot fully evolve out of this earth plane of existence, as a full-fledged god, until you have also loved your own physical body into that divine state of sublime existence with you!

Meanwhile, your soul mate will also love your incredible body, in equal measure to your own loving and tending care for it, and vice versa. That blissfully loving touch of the hand of your soul mate will justify any and all efforts you now put into loving your own body. Then, when the two of you meet and merge in the ecstasy of that union, you will happily discover that he or she will love your body, too!

24

The Magnetism of Joy

Joy is more than just a human emotion, it has an immense magnetic quality. In fact, nothing is more attractive to a normal human being than the vibratory tone of joy! Joy has an incredible attracting power. Joy lights up the landscape in all directions and draws the attention of your eye.

By increasing joy in your being, you increase your power and your speed of drawing your soul mate to you! So through your understanding of joy and your intelligent efforts toward accelerating joy in your own being, you can materialize your soul mate into your life much faster. At the same time, you increase your mental, emotional and physical health tremendously.

Your pituitary gland, the master gland of your body, is light activated. Joy is a very high and rapid vibration that attains the speed of light and triggers your pituitary to *open* your brain.

You will note in stark contrast that people who are the most joyless are the ones with the most closed, or the tightest shut brains! It is extremely difficult for them to acknowledge new things because their brains are not open.

Joy also activates your intuition, your psyche, or psychic abilities. Joy literally allows you to be more in touch with the world and your comrades around you.

Joy alters your hormones and the speed of electrical firing through the neural system of your entire brain structure. Joy encourages harmony and a subsequent health to your whole being.

Joy keeps your body from aging like no other "additive" in your system. When your whole structure feels joy and harmony, disease is impossible!

Joy works through your pituitary controls and balances your blood pressure.

Joy is the one singular tremendously high vibration that is tolerated or withstood by your body. Joy works to restore natural rhythm. Joy is initially registered or felt in your "heart-mind" solar plexus area.

Joy adds fluid and dynamic vitality to your physical and mental being. Joy uplifts you to the very "highest heavens" of your existence. Joy ushers in a sense of peace and a sublime state of relaxation in every cell of your body.

Joy is one of the rare few essences of life that you cannot get too much of in any part of, or anywhere in your whole human system.

The question now then is how do you generate or create more joy in your life, and even more specifically, in your own self?

Fortunately, there are several easy ways to achieve this. Your solar-plexus "mind"—the gray matter in your solar plexus—was specifically designed to facilitate the receivership of more sensation or feeling in your body. The more you feel, the more chemicals you trigger that are needed by your "interpretive" brain.

Essentially, the first human brain created was the primate brain. It is similar in function to all animal brains. Even an earthworm has this brain! It runs your biological body.

The second human brain created was your "light" brain and was added later to facilitate light coming in from your light entity self now within the human body.

The third human brain is the "interpretive" brain out of which the intellect was born in humanity.

The fourth human brain created was your "solar-plexus" brain, added to receive and accelerate feeling, which allows the interpretive mind to link all four brain systems together, operating them all simultaneously as a whole!

The average human being only experiences rare and meager states of joy throughout an entire lifetime. This is never enough to open the brain fully and make a superman or superwoman out of you. However, it can be done through prolonged or extended states of great joy. That full charge of electricity awakens and utilizes every single cell of your body to bring you into the range of super power and super creativity!!

Usually, your states of joy rarely last more than a few minutes. You can intentionally generate and feel a growing and sustained joy through your fourth brain area—the solar-plexus-mind. All vibrations or feelings of joy must initially pass through this region in order to access your body.

Your "feeling tone" of joy cannot be faked. It must be genuine. No amount of "lip service" will attain it. Only your sincere feelings of elation, of appreciation, of reverence, or whatever other emotional catalyst that you uniquely need or desire to "psyche you up" into a high and sustained feeling of joy will work!

In your effort to cultivate joy, note that the greatest genuine joy is generated from subtle, rather than gross stimulation. Some of your greatest thrills in all life come from hearing the classical music of the great composer masters, or seeing a sublime sunrise or sunset, or catching a glimpse of the Grand Canyon, the star-studded night sky, or other panoramas of exquisite sensual stimuli.

It may take you a period of five or ten minutes to get deep enough to bypass those tingling worry or "entrainment vibrations" at the surface, and through several of the layers of your body mass. However, the effort will be worth it. When you find that "gentle space" within your being, your body will resonate with joy. Your magnetic level will rise and you can start "broadcasting" your location to your soul mate. The result of that increased magnetic field is increased attraction—you attract or draw your soul mate to you much more quickly!

When you and your soul mate merge together, your joy more than doubles. The combined amount of joy is equivalent to the square of two—or, four times as much joy felt by each one of you!

This accounts for another reason why soul mates coupled together evolve much quicker than singles. Their great joy together consumes, enriches, and is re-given, again and again, between both of them.

Go deep into your self and simply acknowledge your own great excitement for life! Use meditation, contemplation, or whatever works best for you to accelerate your feelings of joy. I already know the joy of a grand soul mate relationship. May that sublime joy of creating, attracting, and knowing a divine soul mate relationship be yours soon!

25

What Is Love?

Most individuals are asking the question, where is love, without knowing what is love! Most of the heterosexuals, as well as most homosexuals or bisexuals, will be surprised to know that love has nothing to do with sex. The lust for sex activity is, in fact, just the opposite of genuine love—since it consists of wanting to possess, or taking.

Love is giving!

The first universal "act of love" was when the great source of all that is gave itself to be a universal canvas, stage, or platform for ensuing life existences to spring forth into being. This Law of Love, or Law of Giving initiated the first universal extension of dimension and movement and began a rhythmic-balanced-interchange without end! This first act of love given was re-given back to the source, only to be given and re-given again and again, endlessly. This piston-like movement of expansion-compression is the cause of all cosmic motion and life expression. Pure love is pure giving with no conditions attached!

Conditional "love" was created by human beings, not by the source. The very act of demanding love is the exact opposite of love. Love never demands, it gives. Love can only be received and re-given.

When soul mates, or any other interchanging pairs, or mates give equally to each other, their lives are not only filled and fulfilled with love, but also with balance and an ongoing harmonious and rhythmic interchange.

This great Law of Love—of giving and re-giving—applies equally between seller and buyer, brother and sister, mother and daughter, race and race, country and country, etc. Once established with a given civilization, it will cause worldwide harmony throughout it, or through any other giving and re-giving civilization.

Love is obviously not taking! Taking is the opposite of love exactly. Love received becomes validated only when re-given equally in return. The true lover gives and wants nothing extra in return. The taker, on the other hand, acts contrary to universal life flow. He or she is pushing up against a strong river flow. The taker eventually loses all taken, while the giver is re-given more!

When all humankind fully understand this principle of a giving love—one that is not possessive or conditional—it will blossom out of the Age of Slaughter into The Golden Age of divine harmony, of rhythmic-balanced-interchange!

As an enlightened soul mate that knows and lives this law of giving, you will be a visible forerunner of that new birthing of The Golden Age of earth. Your giving, loving, caring, lives will "seed" your genes and give your offspring with new levels of love and understanding, too.

Love is by far the greatest treasure that anyone can gift another—because it is the gift of self. Your own proximity to another is your statement of love to them, as well. To give love to another is the beginning of a genuine love life, for what you give to another is re-given back to you!

You must first give you your love, then you will have it to give to another. Self love is needed before you own the love to give to your soul mate and to others. When your own love of self literally "brims over," then you have a great surplus of love to re-give freely and generously to your soul mate.

Love is also a life of action. An actionless life is a loveless life! Any act of movement toward self-fulfillment denotes love of self. Think it through!

On the other hand, it is obvious that a drowning person who does not "struggle for life" does not love himself or herself. A person who "stalemates" himself or herself, by constantly "sitting on the fence" displays a lack of love for self, too. Love is your gift to you—of wise action toward joyful expression and a pleasant continuity of your life. I suggest you begin to now love yourself even more by taking all of this knowledge and acting on your desire to materialize your soul mate in your life!

26

The Love and Joy of a Soul Mate Relationship

Once you have tasted the honey of a soul mate relationship, you will not settle for the taste of vinegar and of dry, gray ashes of loneliness or rejection anymore!

Once you have touched the presence and bonded with your soul mate, you will stop looking and feasting on other sexual "attractions." All that you want and need in every way, including sex, is now at hand!

There is much love and joy shared between soul mates, but when any two strong individuals interact, there must be conflicts and compromises. No two individuals will always agree on the same thing!

Soul mates are able to fully trust each other, so they can allow themselves to be open and vulnerable in their interactions with each other. This reduces conflict.

Think about it. Nothing feels so good as being able to be yourself, anywhere, anytime! When you can be perfectly honest with your mate, and he or she knows complete honesty with you—all of the great walls of inhibition come tumbling down. Both of you can freely express all your deepest and truest feelings to one another soul mate without any fear or embarrassment. His or her body vibrates at the same frequency as your own, so you understand him or her like no other—and vice versa.

Psychologically, as well as physically, soul mates who are both secure in their spirits are well matched. Thus, they usually find full agreement in most things. Their disagreements are normally few and far between—and almost all of those end in *mutual* compromise.

However, anyone can change for the better or worse. So if one of the bonded soul mates degenerates, or fails to keep growing with the other, the relationship will end. If the imbalance is too prolonged, it would break the bond between them—and usually it leaves a huge gap in both of their individual beings! That is rare, most soul mates can weather the many storms of life with ease.

Sexually, to soul mates the thrill of touching, of loving and worshipping and merging the bodies of each other—and of holding great respect and honor for the divine god within those blessed bodies of each other is blissful beyond words!

Theirs is no mere mundane involvement, or "one night stand." It is another page lived of an everlasting love story, unmatched by any previous normal love affairs! It is a love divine in scope and beyond mere fantasy.

However, nothing in the universe is forever! Soul mates are mated during their incarnations together—and each relationship will last through that lifetime or end at some point; it is not forever. The rare exception is when the two fully self-realized entities merge back into one light entity again.

Meanwhile, a soul mate forever fantasy is just that—a wishful fancy with no true existence in reality. Nature never gets "stuck" or bogged down in any one place or time for long.

For those whose lofty ideals of "a soul mate forever" are dashed, there is that other brighter side of the coin—total merger of you and your soul mate into one! However, I personally know of no two soul mates who are both ready for that. Theoretically, in time, if soul mates are together long enough, they would naturally keep vibrating closer and closer to each other until they did merge into one light being.

On a short term basis—this is not possible unless both soul mates are willing and able to surrender total identity of self *as a unit of one*! My own attitude is go for it! All of us must eventually make that great transformation, so why not sooner than later?

Soul mates who achieve this rare one-identity merger are on their way toward becoming the ultimate ONE that each of us will ultimately become. How do you do it? By being secure enough to personally release all identities, one by one, until no more exist, other than the two ones NOW pooled into ONE.

A soul mate relationship is filled with exquisite love and joy, and personal self-growth is greatly accelerated. I have one, and I highly recommend that everyone seeks out and experiences that kind of a blissful wedding of two beings, in this lifetime. Your biological soul mate is in your genes. He or she is that close already. You only need to focus him or her into your arms. May the great "force" inside and outside your genes be with you!

27

What about Bisexuality?

Our entire focus up to this point has been on homosexuality and heterosexuals, but what about bisexuals? Do they have soul mates?

Not only do bisexuals have soul mates, but their odds of finding them appear to be double! They can go either way—male or female—to find sexual fulfillment.

Bisexuals are a very tiny percentage of the great mass of homosexual and heterosexual lovers, but they do exist, and are to be loved, honored, and respected the same as any other human being. I have met a few bisexuals in my lifetime and I have found each one of them to be especially loving, allowing, and beautiful souls.

Bisexuality springs from the same genetic pools and DNA held in homosexuals and heterosexuals. It is just as natural a sex drive as yours, or mine, or anyone else's. Bisexuals are doing their thing, and deserve to be allowed to continue doing so.

A bisexual has soul mates the same as anyone else, as well. The principle works the same for them. They can focus in and draw a mirror image of self to them if the desire and focus is strong enough and persistent enough! Soul mates always want to be loved as much as you want to love them, so they are willing and eager to be found.

For the uninformed, bisexuals are not asexual. They are not people with two different sex organs. They are rare individuals, either male or female, that can truly find sexual fulfillment with the opposite sex, or with their own sex—and obviously, are highly sexed. They enjoy sex immensely and achieve satisfaction going either way—with alternating current, or direct current.

Of course, the most balancing soul mate for a bisexual would be another bisexual. Here again the union can be with either male or female. Like the rest of us, bisexuals will be around for a long time. If you encounter one, don't be afraid. They respect your right to preference the same as you can kindly respect theirs!

28

The Soul Mate Materialization Technique

As you gather more knowledge about creation or creating, for creation is not static, but ongoing—you will understand why "The chicken came before the egg!" The whole of anything is always created first, then the parts are filled in or overlaid.

In all creations, subsequent physical materialization follows that same identical process. The entire known and unknown universe began first as the whole idea of it, then all of it was gradually filled in!

The greatest known scientist of the 19th century, Nikolas Tesla, understood this process fully. He was the young man that introduced alternating current electricity to the world. A jealous Thomas Edison fought to prove that his invention of direct current was superior, but Tesla easily demonstrated publicly that alternating current could be transmitted anywhere across the world, with, or without electrical wires!

J. P. Morgan, in the interests of the elite power brokers did all he could to quickly bury the "free energy" machines invented by Tesla. That knowledge, and even the memory of Tesla, was deliberately obscured and hidden as much as possible, so that scientific public use of free energy could not be developed and used by the masses, keeping us in the dark ages needlessly.

Tesla had the unique faculty to mentally create his inventions in his mind first, as a finished product. He could "run" the machine or invention in his mind and would know which parts of the machine were weak and would wear out or break first. He not only understood, but practiced the art of creating from the end to the beginning, masterfully!

Only one other spiritual giant, Walter Russell, knew, understood and even taught this creativity technique. He, too, has been obscured and kept hidden from the public by the power brokers who have marketed earth-polluting oil instead!

Your own ability to comprehend and utilize natural universal materialization techniques will enable you to not only materialize your longed for soul mate, but anything else you strongly desire, as well. Therefore, sit back and learn it well!

To keep "perpetual motion" a secret, and to keep this natural creative method a secret, we have deliberately been taught that we must start to build anything from the beginning. Then gradually our creation becomes finished and whole. We have been taught to think from the specific to the general, from the particular to the whole all of our growing lives. Now we must reverse that way of thinking. Instead, we need to learn how to withdraw from the immediate and find the overview, or whole approach to the picture. Our train of thinking must move from the whole to the part, from the general to the specific. We need to assume the perspective that our own life force and motion flows from the whole to the part. It puts us back into proper perspective. Instead of the toenail telling the body what to do, the body tells the toenail what to do.

Let us now begin this process by using your soul mate as the ideal you wish to create or materialize in your life. There are billions of "models" already created in the known universe, so you do not have to step back or reach back into the unknown for this job! It would be silly to start creating him or her at the toenail or any other portion or part of the body. Instead you step back and scan the billions of male models already recorded in your DNA and genetic memory, if you are shopping for a male, and vice versa if you are shopping for a female. There are plenty to choose from, since you can overlay the parts as desired, after the whole form has been chosen. Is he or she big, little, fat, or thin—as an ideal physique or shape? It's your choice! Once that whole form is chosen, you can move on to your choice of color, race, personality, etc., gradually filling in the color of eyes, dimples, and all of the other favorite "parts and pieces." Of course the whole mental process takes place almost in a flash, since your genes already know what you really like!

Here are some of the other almost simultaneous processes you will be involved in with the creation of your soul mate. While building the whole image, you must also sense out the feeling tone of your soul mate—meaning how does the thought and image of him or her in your life loving you make you feel! That feeling tone is his or her own unique pulse or note of identity. It is like tuning in FM 137 on the frequency band specifically, instead of spinning the dial and hoping you will get the station you want to tune in. It is that feeling tone that will sound out to him or her and broadcast your existence and your location so the union can be found and made.

Since you are a "light entity" you work with light! As your model and the parts and pieces take shape in mind, you are building a holographic photo of your soul mate. Once the photo is complete, you hold that holographic image in the light of your mind, combined with the desire wanting to be with him or her, generating the feeling tone of our soul mate simultaneously. That image will be imprinted on the universal canvas, and similar to a negative forming a picture, it will draw all of the "parts and pieces" needed to magnetize molecular and cellular structure to fill in your light structure.

At that point, the entire holographic image of your soul mate forms a vortex of attraction between the physical counterpart of that image and yourself. If you were birthing something new, the image would form a single cell, and placed into the proper medium, grows into the fully matured ideal of what you have created. That is how every butterfly—to elephant—to your human body was initially created.

Your job is easy and a lot of fun! It is like going shopping at a giant soul mate "mart" where every conceivable soul mate is available.

Once you have sorted out your choice of the whole form of your soul mate, be as detailed as you can imagine, for what you put into this image or hologram is what you get! If you receive a few unwanted surprises, it is because you failed to delete that aspect of your soul mate. If pubic nose pickers or anti-social behavior offends you, choose a model that omits those traits and has the physical or esthetic traits that please you instead! If Tesla could fill in all of the right parts of his "invention," to know exactly how it worked, so can you. The more specific you are about how your soul mate looks and feels to you, the greater the magnetism generated between you and the "real thing" when that broadcast goes out on the ethers. That feeling tone also helps you to identify your soul mate immediately when you first meet, and vice versa.

As a creator, you are also working in the time spectrum. You are putting your own "intent package" into time to alter events that conform to your new perspective. You are displacing the events of time with your own intents of time! Which validates that you have now taken charge of your life!

Perspective is another major creative ingredient in materializing your desire. Instead of holding on to the old perspective—even if it is true—that you lacked a soul mate in your life, substitute the feeling and the self-assurance that he or she is finally there with you. Use the "act as if" principle so powerfully that your new perspective will automatically be filled in with the parts and pieces like the black negative gathering molecular form as the picture gathers density when light and chemistry work together. When your perspective is changed, you see the world in a new light and your chemistry changes as well! Instead of loneliness and lack, you feel joy and elation over the prospect that your greatly longed for soul mate will soon be in your arms physically.

Insight into the creation process can be learned from a xerox copy. No matter how pure the "original" copy—if the negative plate you lay the original upon is smudged with ink, the copy you receive will have ink smudges and possibly unreadable copy on it. So be wise enough to use a clear reproduction "machine." A radio reception will also become inaudible and blur words of communication if the static is too loud and strong.

Your body is both a sending and a receiving station. Whether you are aware of it or not, your body is loaded with "static." Therefore, before beaming out your messages or creative frequency wave pulses, it is important to "clear the air."

Stop your train of thought for a moment and feel the subtle vibrations emitted from your body. Those vibrations will be greater or lesser, from moment to moment. Try it. Try it again. And again.

With more practice, you will find you can go into deeper and deeper levels or layers of these vibrations. The outermost ones with the greatest vibration are your "worry entrainment" vibrations. These come from your many daily worries and fears and are continually conditioning your unfolding life events with that same old worryful tone. Therefore, like the xerox machine, you must make sure you have cleared or erased all your "jitters" or worry entrainment vibrations before you begin your materialization process. Otherwise, your new materialization will be discolored and loaded with worry. You do not want your loving soul mate to bring you a load of worry. You want a ton of joy instead, so take the time to clear the air before you focus on materializing that special someone to you!

Manifestation and materialization are also two different things. Manifestation is your process of opening a "gap" or abstract piece of reality—a space that the source can come through to materialize your desire.

Usually, most of us fill our gaps with prolonged and too much intensity of self. That only re-creates a reproduction of the exact same self-situation. The net result is seemingly more struggle.

The gap should be left open, not filled up with your intensity. As the next universal wave washes over your being, your brain will insert your desire, and it will then quickly materialize.

You only need to calm your body and clear your vibratory space down to the most subtle level you can get—then focus the "feeling tone" of your desire into it. Nature, or the source will fill in the empty space. The old scientific adage, "nature abhors a vacuum" is absolutely true.

If you can get down to about six strobing levels or layers of subtlety, you arrive at true self—where an understated joy, or gap exists. Create the biggest gap you can. Hold that gentle calmness as long as you can—free of any manifestation intensity. When both the mental self and feeling self strobe together at the same time, that tone or note you are holding will manifest and subsequently materialize.

The creative waves keep coming so the more gaps you can get to orbit your field, the more materialization opportunities you have. The gaps act like fuel to the brain. They ignite and produce your material desire.

This explains why people who are calm and clear about what they truly want, and who are appreciating and focusing on what pleases them in life, generally get what they want, and it is loaded with pleasure and joy.

Once you feel out this worry entrainment vibration, "rev" it up like you would rev up a car engine—then let go and mentally say "release" or any other word that means let go. As you find each deeper level, rev it up and say your release word mentally. Gradually your brain will "catch on" and will then instantly erase all those worry vibrations whenever you sound out that "let go" order—any time of day or night—without all the preparatory work that you did to calm the body down in the beginning. Self-suggestion is a powerful tool!

Notice that this is a gentle and almost effortless process. When you are in struggle, you are working against nature. Nature always does everything very effortlessly. Nature does not possess a false "human work ethic" or a false struggle ethic! That is manmade. Nature does whatever it does easily, and so can you. Nature is abundant and knows it!

You can not only manifest and bring your soul mate into your life—you can also materialize any amount of the money you want—or anything else you desire with little or no effort! It usually takes only five to ten minutes of time, or less, to create each manifestation gap. Instead of making it work, make it fun! Joy intensifies all creativity.

When you begin carrying that understated joy consciously around with you, no matter how terrible life seems, you are beginning to work at atomic levels, rather than through your hormonal or cellular biology. At that dynamic level, nothing is impossible to you. A mere "pinch" of atoms can create an atomic bomb. When you are running on atomic power, you are operating on high grade, or premium fuel—and your power to manifest and materialize is boundless.

Fear, doubt and guilt can neutralize or completely destroy your manifestation before it can materialize. So be sure to face any doubts, guilts or fears you might be playing around with before you start this materialization process. Your good self-image and the sure knowledge that you choose to live in a safe world will soon dissolve all of those negative thoughts and feelings.

Mind power is awesome! One lady I know has scientifically proven that she can bend a laser beam with a strong focus of her mind. This means *your* mind is more intense and powerful than a laser beam—so use it gently and wisely.

The following seven "mental practices" are condensed from *Finding Your Soul Mate.*

Manifestation Technique

1) Create a clear, uncompromising mental picture of your soul mate, as *desired.* Focus in on him or her with feeling tone several times each day.

2) On a same time of day basis, think lovingly and endearingly toward your soul mate—for at least five minutes every day or night. Then go on with daily life.

3) During this broadcast, tell your soul mate the town or city and country you are living in. He or she will pick up this message at some level of being and will be drawn to your location, or vice versa.

4) Notify your soul mate during this broadcast the day, month, or year you anticipate his or her arrival in your life!

5) Create many vivid pictures in your mind of you with your soul mate going to familiar and romantic places together. Live and feel each exciting experience *together* vividly!

6) Affirm your gratitude at the end of each of your broadcasts—that your desire is fulfilled and your soul mate is close at hand.

7) Give thanks, acknowledging the source as the generous giver of all gifts. Affirm you will re-give all love received from your soul mate back to him or her!

You now have most of the known and proven tools to help you attract your soul mate into your life. Let me know how you are doing, in care of this publisher. If you want further clarification on any point I have presented here, ask. We are one!

29

The Age of Soul Mate Mergers

Our planet earth has begun to spin and expand into a whole new dimension of existence. This "new earth" or appearance of earth materializing "higher" knowingness and beingness is definitely aiding the merger, the union, or coming together of soul mate "couples."

This motion of all life on earth toward unity tends naturally at the most elementary levels, to bring two into one! The most normal, conscious, and easiest flow into unity at this time is between soul mates. They already are focused on a mutual wave length—so are most naturally drawn together.

In the magnetic half of the universe, likes are attracted to likes! Sounds like homosexuality, does it not? This "sameness" merging with sameness is why using a gyroscopic principle, grains of sand merge with grains of sand, gravel with gravel, rocks with rocks, gold with gold, etc. All of these differentiated particle units gravitate and merge at their common level or plane of existence. Without this principle you could not find and hold a handful of sand.

A soul mate finds a soul mate the same way, for both of them are essentially the same. Another old adage fits aptly here. "Birds of a feather flock together!" The same picture can be broadened. Criminals hang out together. The "good guys" and "good girls" of course, hang out together, patriots, hunters, educators, etc., for they are all of the same mind!

This new planetary "birth" so widely predicted to occur during our existing generation, will bring real unity among all living human participants in the event. It certainly will not be the projected One World Order, meaning a one world government, ruled by the elite!

When this event reaches critical mass, the planetary nucleus will literally split, dividing into an uplifted securely love based whole—while leaving a material fear based whole behind. All humanoids still stuck in a fear-based reality will also be stuck on the denser planetary body left behind—as the newly birthed earth spirals off into the creation of a new universe of its own! The uplifted inhabitants upon it will go for the "ride of their lives!"

To observers on the fear-based earth left behind it will seem that a whole lot of people have suddenly vanished. To observers on the new earth, they will still be able to see the struggle and chaos involving those left behind on the old earth, but will not be physically effected by it. Their world is safe and secure—just as they have made it! Those individuals and groups in the "higher" dimension of earth will understand why, while those left behind on the "lower earth" will be confused at first, but will go on with their fear-based lives and will rely on their myths to explain away what happened.

Meanwhile, every single one of us on earth is being altered, more pronounced and uplifted as wave upon wave of this coming new birth vibrations washes over and transforms us a little more with each persistent wave.

Since that whole thrust is toward unifying likes toward likes, soul mates are awakening , aroused with the desire to be with someone of a similar tone, note, or nature! The very fact that you were drawn into reading this book indicates you have awakened to the "signal."

My own conscious role in this drama is to present this knowledge and the techniques to you. This allows you to speed up the process of drawing your soul mate into physical proximity with you!

As you and I, and other countless soul mates merge together, the process "quickens" until that point when critical mass is reached, when the final actual planetary nucleus split occurs!

The question is where will you be when this awesome division happens? Where is your consciousness now? Will you master your body and move into the greater future and dimension with your own self, or with your soul mate? Or, will you allow fear and low self-esteem to keep you pinned to the old fear-based earth to be left behind?

There is nothing to fear physically, or in any way from this magnificent, long-awaited and imminent birthing event! If you are in a state of fear, discover why! If you are in a state of joy and truly love yourself, you are absolutely assured of moving forward into the higher dimension. This is a "do it yourself" job. No one is coming to do it for you, though there will be, of course, divine intervention, where needed, and when needed, as always happens under unusual circumstances. So if you love you, no matter where you are—even in the eye of a hurricane—when the planetary split occurs, you will make a safe transition from this fear-based earth to the new love based earth!

Where will you be? Only you know! It's your choice. I know you will choose wisely. Bless you and bless your most beloved soul mate. We will meet again. I love you!

Michael

Suggested Reading and Other Sources

Alexander, Thea. *Twenty-One Fifty A.D.* Tempe, AZ: Macro Books, 1971.

Bailey, Alice A. *A Treatise on Cosmic Fire.* New York: Lucis Trust, 1951.

Blavatsky, Helena P. *Isis Unveiled.* Wheaton, IL: Theosophical Society, 1976.

———. *The Secret Doctrine.* Wheaton, IL: Theosophical Society, 1980.

Bryce, Sheridan. *Joyriding the Universe.* Homewords Publishing, n.d. (Box 57396, Salt Lake City, UT 84157).

Carey, Ken. *Vision.* Kansas City, MO: Uni-Sun, 1988.

Cayce, Edgar. There are many books by and about Edgar Cayce and his work. The following were written by Edgar Cayce and are recommended: *Auras.* Virginia Beach, VA: A.R.E., 1945; *Edgar Cayce on Atlantis.* New York: Warner, 1988; *Revelation.* Virginia Beach, VA: A.R.E., 1969; *A Search for God, V2.* Virginia Beach, VA: A.R.E., 1950; *Think on These Things: Selections from the Edgar Cayce Readings.* Virginia Beach, VA: A.R.E., 1981. Books by other authors: *The Edgar Cayce Handbook for Health* by Harold Reilly and Ruth Brod. Virginia Beach, VA: A.R.E., 1975; *Edgar Cayce's Story of the Soul* by W. H. Church. Virginia Beach, VA: A.R.E., 1989; and *There is a River* by Thomas Sugrue. Virginia Beach, VA: A.R.E., 1942.

Light Speed. Earth Mission Publishing (P.O. Box 956#0432, Kihei, HI 96753). This organization offers a free newsletter and many "earth star" video, audiotapes, books and seminars.

Michael. *Finding Your Soul Mate.* York Beach, ME: Samuel Weiser, 1992.

Monroe, Robert. *Far Journeys.* New York: Doubleday, 1987.

Paramahansa Yogananda. *Autobiography of a Yogi.* Los Angeles: Self-Realization Fellowship, 1981.

The Phillip Material. Homewords Publishing (Box 57396, Salt Lake City, UT 84157).

Ramtha. *Ramtha.* Eastsound, WA: Sovereignty, 1986.

Roberts, Jane. *How to Develop Your ESP Power.* New York: Simon & Schuster, 1986.

———. *The Seth Material.* New York: Bantam, 1976.

Roberts, Jane and Richard Roberts. *The Seth Reader: The Essence of the Wisdom of Seth Selected in Chronological Order from the Seth Works of Jane Roberts.* San Anselmo, CA: Vernal Equinox, n.d.

Russell, Walter. *The Secret of Light.* Waynesboro, VA: University of Science & Philosophy, 1974.

Dr. Michael is the author of ten self-improvement books. He is a former professional basketball player, published songwriter, television host of his own series, *The Mysteries of Life*, and has taught psychology at the University of Humanistic Studies in San Diego, California. In 1984, he was awarded the distinguished Bronze Halo Award by The Southern California Motion Picture Council, for his contribution as an author, lecturer, philanthropist, and humanitarian. He is the author of *Finding Your Soul Mate* also published by Samuel Weiser.